A Black Girl's Guide
COLLEGE BOUND
Everything You Need to Know Before Starting College

A Black Girl's Guide

COLLEGE BOUND

EVERYTHING YOU NEED TO KNOW BEFORE STARTING COLLEGE

Rahkal C. D. Shelton

Copyright © 2023 by Connect Create Inspire

All rights reserved. This book or any portion thereof may not be reproduced or used in any manner whatsoever without the express written permission of the publisher except for the use of brief quotations in a book review or scholarly journal.

Printed in the United States of America

ISBN: 978-1-7376892-4-9

Rahkal C. D. Shelton
Lawrenceville, Georgia 30043

College Bound
www.rahkalshelton.com

Bible versions used:

The Passion Translation® (TPT). Copyright © 2017, 2018, 2020 by Passion & Fire Ministries, Inc. Used by permission. All rights reserved. ThePassionTranslation.com.

GOD'S WORD Translation (GW). Copyright © 1995, 2003, 2013, 2014, 2019, 2020 by God's Word to the Nations Mission Society. All rights reserved.

Holy Bible, New International Version®, NIV® Copyright ©1973, 1978, 1984, 2011 by Biblica, Inc.® Used by permission. All rights reserved worldwide.

Common English Bible (CEB). Copyright © 2011 by Common English Bible.

The Message (MSG). Copyright © 1993, 2002, 2018 by Eugene H. Peterson.

Disclaimer: While the author uses some biblical references and commentary from a Christian perspective, she understands that not every belief expressed in this book aligns with readers' thoughts. Therefore, it is highly recommended that readers (with different views) focus on the well-researched, accurate information, strategies, and principles geared toward college prep and career readiness.

DEDICATION

To my dearest niece, Jada, and every brown and Black girl I've had the pleasure of coaching or mentoring, thank you for letting me be a part of your journey. I pray you will pay it forward.

AUTHOR'S NOTE

Hey, little sis, I'm thrilled you're reading this book! It's been a long time coming, too. My idea for *College Bound* came to me back in 2009, a couple of years after finishing my bachelor's in '07. If you're just turning 16 or 17 years old, this probably sounds like forever ago.

Well, life has been life'n, and I've been kind of busy mentoring, working, teaching, and publishing other books, but also better preparing for this moment to deliver my very best to you. My name is Rahkal Shelton Roberson, but you can call me Big Sis, Aunty Rahky, or Coach Rahk. I am a mentor, certified professional life coach, college and career readiness expert, and career strategist.

In short, I help women and young women like yourself have healthy and happier lives personally and professionally. And can I tell you something? I absolutely LOVE what I do! I have no doubt that God created me with a deep passion and purpose to serve and mentor young women. What makes me qualified to write this book? Well, a few things: I have worked in a college/career prep capacity for over fourteen years and have worked with students in school districts in Houston, Atlanta, DC, and Chicago as a tutor, lead instructor, mentor, speaker, or college prep coach.

My heart for serving women includes nonprofit work, speaking engagements, and community outreach programs where I facilitated, coached, and mentored teens, providing me opportunities to build and forge trusting relationships with young women. And then there are my personal life experiences. I was the first in my family to graduate from high school and the first in my family to attend college more than twelve hours away. My mother was a former drug addict who dropped out of ninth grade and raised me in a single-parent household. It was a blessing that we left my father just before I started kindergarten. I grew up in a very toxic environment, witnessing my parents' drug use and my father's violent behavior, which devastated my mother and our family.

HIGH SCHOOL GRADUATION
(granny, me, and mama)

However, due to my mother's courage, we escaped my father's control. So, I was raised without him and by a mother with limited education. I remember wishing I had more support, a mentor, or someone at home to help with school and to think through what would come next in life. As a Black girl from the inner city who grew up in low-income housing with limited resources and exposure and whose family moved frequently, I simply did what I could.

Despite this, I had one thing going for me: determination and a fighting spirit that remained defiant. My mother is where I got my fighting spirit. And I yearned for experiences beyond the limited scope of my upbringing. Going to college was my escape plan.

Many of my lessons were learned through trial and error and the hard way. From a humiliating senior-year breakup (just before prom), bumming the ACT with an embarrassing score of 12 on the retake (a single point higher than my first attempt), not getting into the school I wanted, not affording application fees, trying to apply for scholarships but being a terrible writer, forging new friendships, freshman-year roommate drama, worrying about my family while away in college, deciding on a major, the Freshman 15, losing my housing and accruing significant credit card and student loan debt; my college experience could have truly broken me. I'm glad it didn't. Those adversities provided me with a solid foundation to build on. Those challenges helped shape me and fueled my desire to serve and support young girls like you.

You may already have a mother, mentor, aunt, or grandmother encouraging you through this process. Or maybe you're the first person in your family to believe you can go to college and are trying to figure things out on your own. Whether you're a teen mom, a barely passing student, a star athlete, a straight-A student, or a homecoming queen, please understand that good and lasting things in life will never be easy!

Because you're a Black woman, you'll have to work for everything, sometimes even harder. Not only will you have to work hard to get what you want, but you'll have to work even harder to keep it. But guess what? You are not required to do it alone. That is why I am here. I'd like to share some of this burden with you by providing you with the cheat code and assisting you in navigating this process more effectively and efficiently. I truly want you to succeed in all aspects of your life. I have faith in you, and I hope you do as well.

And how can anyone preach unless they are sent? As it is written: "How beautiful are the feet of those who bring good news!" —Romans 10:15.

XO,
Coach Rahk

TABLE OF CONTENTS

Author's Note... vii
Acknowledgments..xv
Introduction..xvii

Chapter One: Identity...23
Tangible vs. Intangible..25
Loving, and Leveraging Your Diversity...........................30
Defining the Woman You Want to Be............................34

Chapter Two: Junior and Senior Year Checklist..........39
Goal Setting..42
Junior Year Checklist/Focus by Semester.....................52
Senior Year Checklist/Focus by Semester 56

Chapter Three: College, Universities, Trades, Entrepreneurship........63
Difference Between Colleges, College Types and Universities............65
HBCU and PWI Survival Checklist..................................77
Importance of Having a Skill or Trade...........................84
Entrepreneurship for Black Girls.....................................87

Chapter Four: School Selections and the Application Process..........97
How to Choose Your School and Major.....................100
Lower/Higher Paying Majors/Career Fields................104
How to Apply: The Application Process.....................119

Chapter Five: Paying for College, Side Hustles. Financial Freedom...123
Wealth Gap: Why Blacks Are Behind Financially........124
How to Pay for College: Financial Aid Options..........126
Scholarship Money..131
Side Hustles, Avoiding Debt and Saving......................139
Importance of Credit, Budgeting and Money Management 142

Chapter Six: The Summer Before..159
Traditional Student Summer Checklist.......................................160
Untraditional Student Summer Checklist 165
College Freshman Purchase List..167

Chapter Seven: Orientation, Class Selection, Grad Plans
             and The First Semester.................................169
Sample Graduation Plan..174
Surviving the First Few Weeks and Semester..............................179
Staying Balanced and Ahead First Semester................................182
Career Tips for a Successful First Year.....................................186

Chapter Eight: Keeping Your Grades Up and
             Time Management.......................................189
How to Stand Out and Be a High Performer.............................190
Time Management Strategies 197
Avoiding Distractions and Procrastinations................................204

Chapter Nine: Woosah, Stress Management and Balance............209
Depression and Anxiety in College..211
Signs of Burnout/Stress Management.......................................217
Self-Care and Boundary Setting Tips.......................................219
Resilience in College...226

Chapter Ten: Relationship Management, Communicating
             and Resolving Conflict..................................229
Relationship Types and Importance...231
Managing and Resolving Conflict...234
Navigating Conflict with Roommates.......................................236
Effective Communication Strategies..239
Making Friends in College...241

Chapter Eleven: Navigating Campus, The Social Scene
                and Going Home..249
Safety Tips for Women in College..251
The Yard/Quad/Campus and Social Scene................................253
Joining Organizations, Clubs and Greek Life..............................254
Visiting Home 260
Setting Boundaries With Loved Ones.....................................264

Chapter Twelve: Life Beyond College, Career Readiness............267
Making the Most of Senior Year...268
Senior Year Checklist...269
Networking, Mentors and Advocates.....................................270
Career Readiness..273
Planning the Next and Adulting..280
Student Loans..283

Conclusion...285

About the Author...289

ACKNOWLEDGMENTS

Many wonderful people contributed in countless ways to my passion for mentorship and college and career readiness. First and foremost, I'm grateful to be in a relationship with Jesus Christ, my Lord and Savior. Apart from him, I am and can do nothing! I want to acknowledge Vivian Hapaniewski, Tiana Lane, Lakia Marion, and the incredible women at GLOSS Sisterhood. I would also like to thank every young woman whose presence I've had the privilege to encounter, whether coaching, serving, mentoring, from small groups, or just loving on me. Thank you. To my sister and brother, Andre and Rachel Taylor, thank you for allowing me to have a hand in your babies' lives. To my extraordinary husband, Dr. Joe L. Roberson Jr., thank you for your continuous support and selfless sacrifice, being my cheerleader, believing in me, and helping unlock my greatest potential. I love me some you.

INTRODUCTION
WHY THIS BOOK AND HOW TO USE IT

If you're reading this book, you're likely planning to attend college or looking for insight or direction on your next move after high school. Perhaps your mom, dad, or a relative bought you a copy. Maybe you took time off to raise a baby or work a job and are considering returning to school. Wherever you are, don't worry, I got you! You're in the right place and reading the right book!

As a Black woman, first-generation college graduate, mentor, and inner-city youth advocate, I deeply understand the value and importance of inclusion, access, and academic preparedness. This is why I believe Black girls need supplemental college readiness materials. Most mainstream college prep books do not explicitly address the unique challenges, issues, and social/emotional learning needs of Black girls transitioning into this phase of young adult life.

My goal is to help you find your way while exposing you to information to help you better create and trailblaze your unique mark and life's journey. As a Black woman, this time is critical for cultivating identities, identifying and owning purpose, developing skills, and learning as much as possible to mitigate future risks of intersectionality (racism, sexism, inequalities, and other disadvantages) that could create unnecessary obstacles in your future.

Transitioning out of high school can be challenging, scary, a little overwhelming, and exciting all at once, especially for us Black girls, regardless of whether you are in ninth grade or in your senior year, whether you are the first in your family to attend college, a teen mom, or a girl from the hood.

According to studies, Black women are more likely to encounter frustration and opposition in the workplace. Frequently, we are underpaid, overlooked for promotions, discriminated against, stereotyped, harassed due to our hairstyles and Blackness, and undervalued. How does this apply to you? Well, someday, when you graduate college and get into the professional workforce, you must be aware of the obstacles you may face as a Black woman.

Here's a little context. Research also shows that Black high school students have a lower graduation rate. According to findings by The Brookings Institute and The National Center for Education Statistics, Black students' on-time high school graduation rate in most states is even lower than white, Asian/Pacific Islander, and Hispanic students. This means if Black students barely graduate from high school, they're even less likely to attend college, gain a skill, or become successful.[1]

You're probably thinking, *why is this?* Much of it is due to economic and social disadvantages in our communities, including poverty, single-parent/lower-income households, and a lack of access to basic necessities like food and hot water, especially for those living in extreme poverty. Teen pregnancy, inferiority complexes, discriminatory disciplinary actions like Black kids being expelled and suspended from school more than white kids (for small offenses), and lack of support, exposure, and motivation all play a crucial role in the probability of Black students' success in the classroom and life after high school.

---

[1] Richard V. Reeves and Simran Kalkat, "Racial disparities in the high school graduation gender gap," Brookings, April 18, 2023, https://www.brookings.edu/articles/racial-disparities-in-the-high-school-graduation-gender-gap/.

INTRODUCTION

So, what can you do? First, you can finish reading this book and decide what impact you want to make on your community, family, culture, and the world. The next thing you can do is work on making your impact and motivate your friends to do the same and finish school.

My goal is to be completely honest with you regarding some of the adversities you will soon face and remind you how resilient, intelligent, loved, and gifted you are. How do I know this? For starters, you're reading this book, and that says a lot about you and the type of woman you're preparing to become.

I pride myself on advocating for the underdog, the disenfranchised, underrepresented, underprotected, and the one typically counted out. And in the world we're currently living in, that person is the Black woman. So, I wrote this book to help Black girls better prepare for their futures.

Please use this book as a catalyst to shatter glass ceilings, crush stereotypes, and silence doubters. And always remember that no matter how things appear, there isn't a single thing you can't do or accomplish when you put your mind to it, put hard work behind it, have faith in focus, and trust in God.

These next four to six years of your life will be some of the most challenging but exciting years you'll ever experience. As you prepare for this next season in life, please know that no one is coming to save you, and success is a choice that requires discipline and one that's up to you. Many of you will be setting out into the world solo for the first time. You won't have Daddy, Mama, Auntie, or Big Mama to cook for you, do your laundry, or tell you when to go to bed. All this will be up to you as a college student, and you'll be on your own.

For some, this sounds terrifying; for others, it may sound like you finally have some freedom. However, please know that freedom comes with a price called responsibility. You'll have to learn to make wise decisions, hold down the fort and your living expenses, make your own appointments, juggle classes and your personal and social life, study, and manage your time well.

It sounds like a lot, right? And it can be, but remember, you'll be totally equipped for the challenge and not truly alone! God is with you, and so am I. I believe He sent this book your way, and He'll send real friends, mentors, and additional support to help you along this new journey. As you prepare for life beyond high school, and after reading this book, you'll be ahead of the game and fully equipped to make the most of whatever you decide.

You'll learn so much about yourself and how to select and apply for schools. We will go over career paths, financial literacy, how to handle conflict, discovering your passions, and better identifying your voice and purpose. You'll learn career options, how to advocate for yourself, and how to make connections that will last a lifetime. Most importantly, you will learn to gain independence and begin laying the foundation for the type of woman you want to be and the legacy you'll leave behind.

In this book, we'll cover everything you need to know before starting college and the best practices to shine and do well. I'll share some of my personal stories, laced with lessons, things I wish I knew, and points to ponder. After reading, fully engaging with, and understanding this book, you will be exceptionally prepared and far ahead of the curve.

And the cool thing is that by implementing what you'll learn, you'll set the future 22-to-25-year-old you up for INCREDIBLE success.

From rocking out your junior and senior year checklist to creating healthy study habits, getting scholarships, and creating positive self-care routines, once you finish this book, you'll be equipped to thrive and position yourself as a leading

INTRODUCTION

authority for life after high school and college. The future you will be so proud. Are you ready, little sis?

Let's goooooo!

CHAPTER ONE
IDENTITY

Y ou are the light of the world. A city on top of a hill can't be hidden. Neither do people light a lamp and put it under a basket. Instead, they put it on top of a lampstand, and it shines on all who are in the house. In the same way, let your light shine before people so they can see the good things you do, and praise your Father who is in heaven.
— Matthew 5:14-16, CEB

Before diving deep into what you need to know before starting college, it is imperative to first talk about character. As a young Black woman preparing to enter the real world, you must understand what's most important. That is knowing who you are and who you were created to be. I'm not talking about who you feel you are one day, who culture says you are the next day, or who the TikTok challenges say you should be.

Let's take a moment and really think about this. Little sis, do you know who you REALLY are? Have you considered your character and the type of woman you actually want to be? If not, shall we? Here's a little activity.

I want you to think of one or two women you admire. They can be women you don't know personally, ones you've followed on social media or watched on YouTube or TV. Now, think about what you admire or like about them and why, then write it down.

WOMEN I ADMIRE AND WHAT I ADMIRE ABOUT THEM:

Okay, very good. That exercise aimed to get your brain going and to set up the importance of being a woman of noble character and knowing who you are. But first, I want to share a few definitions with you as we think about character and identity.

IDENTITY

Tangible vs. Intangible

1. Something that is *tangible* is something you can see, feel, touch, and that has a physical existence.

2. Something that is *intangible* is something you can't see, feel, or touch, and it does not have a physical existence.

Your *character* is definitely intangible. Character is defined as the mental and moral qualities distinctive to you. Your character aligns with your behavior and personality. It's what attracts people to you, what you dislike in others, and it's truly all you have. Character is the only thing that can't be taken from you.

Think about the things you listed about the women you admire above. Did you list tangible or intangible things? Knowing the difference between the two helps foster your identity and what's important.

Here's an example:

TANGIBLES

CLOTHES AND SHOES
Example: "I like how she dresses."

iPHONES, SAMSUNG, LAPTOPS
Example: "Man, she has all the new phones and technology that comes out."

BAGS AND PURSES
Example: "She has the cutest purses and new bags."

OTHER MATERIAL THINGS
Example: "I like that she keeps her hair and nails done and that she has 100k followers on TikTok."

MONEY
Example: "I like that her family has money, and she can buy whatever she wants."

IDENTITY
INTANGIBLES

HONEST
Example: "I like that she keeps it real, and I can trust her."

KIND/SWEET
Example: "I like how sweet and nice she is towards me."

BEAUTIFUL/PRETTY
Example: "She's such a beautiful person inside and out."

FUNNY
Example: "She is hilarious. I like hanging with her. She always makes me laugh when I'm feeling sad."

LOYAL
Example: "She always has my back, even when I am not around."

INTELLIGENT
Example: "I like how smart she is."

You probably noticed that the tangible items listed above are all based on material things. When you die, you can't take material things with you, but you will be remembered for your intangibles. This is your CHARACTER!

As you prepare to make your mark on the world and grow into womanhood, it's essential to think about your character and who you were created to be. Did you know that God took His time with you, little sis? He uniquely made you, choosing your birthdate, skin tone, height, humor, and even your style. He made you a Black woman on purpose, and He didn't make you by mistake. And as a Black woman, you're graced with an undeniable elegance, style, rich heritage, perspective, and strength. This is your diversity and how others get to experience your uniqueness. However, if you hide what you've been given, attempt to be someone else, or shrink back your personality, the world can't learn from you. Your perspective and uniqueness are valuable. Please don't allow a fear of being judged, society, or the unfortunate disease of racism to make you feel like you don't belong.

Not only did God make you Black on purpose, but you also weren't a surprise to Him. Your mother may have been surprised by her pregnancy with you, but God allowed her to carry you on purpose. And guess what? He created you for something GREAT, with unique skills and talents that NO ONE, absolutely NO ONE, can do like you.

This is because they ain't you, will never be you, and there is only one you. So, for this reason, it's important to avoid comparing yourself to other girls. You are your competition, and you will never be anyone else because you're too busy being you. You've got your own awesome things going. So get comfortable falling in love with and learning YOU.

However, if you feel weird at times or like you don't fit in, that is because you were created to stand out. You weren't designed to fit in or to try and be like everyone else. Think about this: eagles fly and soar, chickens don't, and eagles don't hang with chickens. So, embrace whatever quirks you've got going; Your quirk is your **wow** factor. Remember, the opening Scripture in this chapter says no one places a light under a basket or tries to hide it. You shouldn't either! Let your light shine brightly without dimming it.

At the same time, you may still be a teenager who may not know what you're really good at or what your light is YET (I say yet because some day you will). Not knowing your purpose or passions is expected at your age, so don't be too hard on yourself; you will always be discovering and learning new things about yourself. I'm certainly learning new things about myself at 39 years old.

While you may not know everything about yourself yet, I can tell you someone who does. That person is God because He made you. Since He is your Creator, He knows why He created you and what He created you for. And the more you spend time with Him, seeking and asking Him to show you your purpose, He will. He loves you just that much, and your true identity will be found in your relationship with Him.

It's in Christ that we find out who we are and what we are living for. Long before we first heard of Christ and got our hopes up, He had His eye on us, had designs on us for glorious living, part of the overall purpose He is working out in everything and everyone. —Ephesians 1:11-12, MSG

LOVING YOUR DIVERSITY

Take a moment and jot down some things you are NOT. Listing what you're not also helps to identify what and who you are. I'll go first. **Example:** I am not weak, unloved, or ugly.

What about you? List a few things that you are **not**.

Now, little sis, let's take a second inventory of your uniqueness. What are some things people tell you you're good at?

What are some things you know you're good at (it doesn't matter how small and can be anything)?

IDENTITY

What are some things you enjoy doing?

How do you handle stress and anxiety?

What could you do differently with stress and anxiety?

What are some things you really love about yourself?

What areas do you tend to procrastinate in?

What are some things you don't really like about yourself?

Can you change the things you don't like (listed above)? If not, why? If so, how?

If you can't change the things above, how can you learn to love and truly accept them?

IDENTITY

What are some things that get you really excited to talk about, think about, or do?

Identifying things you're good at, enjoy, and like about yourself is an easy way to discover yourself better. And thinking about the things you dislike but **can** change is a great way to challenge yourself to be a better woman. Granted, your likes, dislikes, passions, and exposure will shift with maturity, but your core is yours. The more you know about yourself, the better off you'll be after graduation.

Peer pressure in college can be really tough, even more than in high school, because you'll have more freedom than you're used to at home. You'll be solely responsible for your decisions without Mama, Auntie, Granny, or Daddy there to save you. Consequently, it's important to consider these things before you leave for school.

Your actions and the decisions you make now can impact the 25-year-old you. I know you don't know her yet, but you'll want to ensure you set her up for success and make her proud. The best way to do this is to think long-term, not just in the moment.

Here's a funny story: When I was 16, I snuck over to a friend's house who had another guy friend over. He was way older than us, and he did tattoos. I wanted to get some but didn't have enough money. At that time, I wanted to get some cherries tatted on my chest and other tats on my back, arm, and neck.

I am so glad I didn't have the money and that he refused to do them. The 39-year-old me would have been upset and embarrassed with those tats. I don't even like cherries; that was just a popular tat back then, and now I couldn't imagine having a tat on my chest. If I had gotten all those visible tattoos, I would have probably disqualified myself from specific professional job opportunities that I've had as well. The 16-year-old me would have made a poor decision for the 39-year-old me. I hope what I am saying makes sense.

Within those first few years in college, many young ladies lose themselves because they never stopped to think about who they were or who they wanted to be BEFORE college.

Little sis, your goal should be becoming a woman with great character and integrity! Integrity keeps you honest and doing the right thing, even when no one is watching. But even when it seems no one is watching, God sees you, and He's always watching and rooting for you to do the right thing.

HAVE YOU THOUGHT ABOUT THE TYPE OF WOMAN YOU WILL BE IN COLLEGE?

IDENTITY

A WOMAN WITH GOOD CHARACTER AND INTEGRITY

HONEST: "I'm not going to cheat on this exam because that's not who I am, and it's not the right thing to do."

TIMELY: "I'll arrive when they asked me to or even a few minutes early to respect other people's time and so I can leave on time."

SELFLESS/CONSIDERATE: "Anything that I get is a blessing and courtesy. No one owes me anything." "Hmm. If I stay out too late, I may disturb my roommate when I come in. My decisions (although mine) can still impact my family and others closest to me."

RESPECTFUL: "Yes, please. Thank you. Let me ask first and check to see if this is okay with them."

EMPATHETIC: "My roommate made a mistake, and now she's really going through it. Let me see if and how I can help her during this tough time."

KEEPING YOUR WORD, COMMUNICATING, BEING RESPONSIBLE:

- Hey, I really don't feel up to going, but because I said I'd support and gave my word, I am going to honor it, and if I absolutely can't make it, I will communicate why and apologize.

- I don't feel like being here, but this isn't about me. I am here to support my girl because this is important to her.

- If I hang out on the campus late tonight, I will stay up later tomorrow to finish my priorities.

A WOMAN WITH POOR CHARACTER NO INTEGRITY

DISHONEST: "The test answers are right here. I need this A, and no one will know if I copy them or not. I'll do it just this one time."

CHRONIC TARDINESS: "I'll get there when I get there."

SELFISH/ENTITLED: "She owes me. They better come through. I'm going to do what I want. It's all about me, what I want, and how I feel."

DISRESPECTFUL: "I don't care, it ain't me. I'm going to do what I want."

APATHETIC: "She did that to herself; that ain't my problem."

FLAKING/POOR COMMUNICATION/WILDING OUT/ETC.:

- I know I said I would be there or do that, but I changed my mind. I don't feel like it and have a lot going on. They'll understand (but you didn't communicate this).

- Being messy, talking about others in their absence, being petty, and gossiping.

- Partying hard, sleeping around, excessive drinking, irresponsible behaviors, taking advantage of others, and manipulating situations and people.

IDENTITY

You see the difference in good vs. bad character? We will dive deeper into some of these examples later when we jump into relationships, how to handle conflict, and how to navigate the social scene. For now, let's consider the type of woman you want to be.

PS. You were created to be a woman of high character and integrity! As you focus on becoming her first, all the other material things you like and want will come your way. Let's write down the type of woman you want to be. I'll go first.

Example: I am a woman who is generous, loving, patient, fabulous, fit, and fine. I don't trip on the small things, and I am charismatic, wise, successful, and wealthy. I am an incredible wife, coach, author, mentor, speaker, and future mother. I am a great friend, supportive of all. I don't engage in drama, pettiness, gossip, or things that are not worth my time and energy. I am a child of God. I am royalty. I am Black excellence.

Your Turn. Write below.
I am:

CHAPTER TWO
JUNIOR AND SENIOR YEAR CHECKLIST

Isn't it funny how you can recall your first day of kindergarten? What about the anxiety and excitement you felt staying up late the night before freshman year? Maybe you rehearsed different scenarios in your head about what the day would bring or texted your girlfriends expressing who you were looking forward to seeing. Perhaps tomorrow is your first day, and you already have your clothing, shoes, and even matching panties laid out and ready to go.

With every new chapter comes new hope, new responsibility, and anticipation. Entering your junior or senior year of high school is no different. Not only is it exciting, but it's also pretty surreal because now you're only one to two summers away from moving out of the house.

The truth is, the older you become, the faster time flies by. You're probably ready to leave the house and gain more freedom and independence at this age. Am I right? Well, I can promise you this: freedom and independence are overrated. They're actually **very** overrated, and in a couple of years, you're going to wish that all you had to do was go to school, be around your annoying parents, and hang with your friends. There will come a time when you'll miss the simplicity and comfort of having a hot meal prepared for you or knowing that you don't have to pay bills by yourself.

Just to be honest, life can be challenging and tough, but it can also be really sweet and soooo rewarding. Life will have ups and downs, ebbs and flows because it's just a part of the process. The trick to winning in life boils down to how we prepare ourselves, view our challenges, and face them. This determines how much we will enjoy life.

I'm sure you want to live a good life, right? We all do, and the secret to living a good life is to prepare (as much as possible) to be disciplined, learn to laugh at yourself, and give yourself some grace. I say give yourself some grace because we'll sometimes do stupid things and make mistakes as humans. But it's about recovering quickly from our mistakes, learning what we can from them, and being better the next time.

You're probably thinking, *what does any of this have to do with a junior and senior year checklist?* I'll tell you. Remember I mentioned the importance of being prepared and how fast time flies? Exactly. So, I'm sharing additional information to help you prepare a bit more because time is ticking.

Think about it like this. As a student, your primary job is to go to school, keep your room clean, be respectful and responsible, do your homework, and do what you're told to do. Sounds simple, right? While it seems pretty simple, I do understand that it can be hard, especially the older you get. As you go through puberty, more of your own ideas, personality, and feelings will come into play. It's like you're growing up but not grown just yet. It can be a weird in-between. You probably struggle with feeling misunderstood by your parents and other adults right now, and you're likely ready for some freedom. Am I right? I get it. I've been a teenager before.

I'll say this: Junior year is arguably the most important year of your entire high school experience. This is the year to handle your business, demonstrating just how responsible you are in

JUNIOR AND SENIOR YEAR CHECKLIST

efforts to gain more independence. Junior year reflects everything you've learned in your first two years. When done correctly, junior year can be a setup for an easier senior year.

"The most common way people give up their power is by thinking they don't have any."
— Alice Walker[2]

As a junior or senior, you have power and an opportunity to leverage that power by being on top of your studies and assignments. The more responsible you decide to be, the easier life will be. When you demonstrate responsibility, you earn more trust from your parents.

If you're not a junior or senior, you can still set some goals for your junior and senior years. Keep reading for now and remember to return to this chapter when you get to junior year.

If you're already a senior, still take a look at the junior year checklist in case there is something that you missed, but focus on your checklist.

I've crafted a couple of pointers to help you set goals (which are really important this year) and a checklist of what you can anticipate over the next two years. Because every school, state, and city differs, use it as a guide, but also be sure to cross-reference items with your counselors. Following this checklist and setting goals is a great starting point to demonstrate responsibility, which can help to earn your parents'/guardians' trust. Use the checklist to help keep you organized and on track and make your life much easier.

---

[2] "Alice Walker: People give up their power by thinking they don't have any," Big Think, Words of Wisdom, October 23, 2014, https://bigthink.com/words-of-wisdom/alice-walker-people-give-up-their-power-by-thinking-they-dont-have-any-2/.

GOAL SETTING

Take a moment and jot down some of your goals and visions of the future you. Answer each question as honestly as possible. Remember to dream big!

Are you attending college?

What do you want to study?

What does being successful mean to you?

Who is one person that you or your family know is successful?

JUNIOR AND SENIOR YEAR CHECKLIST

Why do you think this person is successful?

What do you think successful people do that's different from unsuccessful people?

What would you like to get paid to do as an adult?

What are you naturally good at?

What do people say you're naturally good at?

What areas do you tend to procrastinate in?

What do you really enjoy doing? For example, what would you do for free?

JUNIOR AND SENIOR YEAR CHECKLIST

What is an area you want to challenge yourself to get better in this year?

What does being independent mean to you?

The world would be a better place if YOU did what?

How do you handle stress and anxiety?

How could you handle stress and anxiety differently?

A goal without a plan is only a wish! Smart goals help to create a clear path to reaching goals. Without goals, it can be difficult to determine how to get to college, get a certain job, or anything you want to achieve. **A SMART GOAL** is a carefully planned, clear, and trackable objective. It stands for **S**pecific, **M**easurable, **A**chievable, **R**elevant, and Time-Based.

Specific: Be as clear and specific as possible with what you want to achieve. For example, instead of saying, "I want to be on the cheerleading team," you might say, "I want to be the captain of the cheer team senior year." The narrower your goal, the more you will understand the necessary steps to get there.

Measurable: What proves you are making progress toward your goal? For example, suppose your goal is to be captain of the cheer team. In that case, you might measure progress by making the team, working out, mastering your position, being a leader, and getting the coach's attention. Setting measurables will help you to re-evaluate and make any changes as needed.

Achievable: Have you set an achievable goal? Setting goals you can reasonably accomplish within a certain timeframe will keep you motivated and focused. Using the above example of being the cheer team captain, you should know what's first required and the skills necessary to be the captain. Before you begin working towards a goal, decide whether it is something you can REALLY commit to now or whether there are some extra steps you should work on first to become better prepared.

Relevant: When setting goals for yourself, consider whether or not they are relevant. Do they make sense for you and align with your beliefs and larger, long-term goals? If a goal does not contribute to your bigger dreams, you should rethink it. Ask yourself why the goal is important to you. How will achieving it help you, and how will it contribute to your future dreams?

Time-based: What is your goal's deadline? Putting a timer on it helps to keep you motivated and prioritizing. For example, suppose your goal is to make captain junior year. In that case, you might be working out the summer before and constantly aim to be prepared. Then again, if you haven't achieved your goal in your timeframe, ask yourself what happened and why. Perhaps your timeframe might have been unrealistic, you might have run into unexpected roadblocks, or your goal might have needed to be more achievable.

YEAR'S GOALS
TOP 3 GOALS FOR THE YEAR

List three goals that you'd like to accomplish this year. For each goal, write out how you'll know when you've succeeded.

EXAMPLE GOAL: To be more productive at school.

I'LL KNOW I'VE SUCCEEDED WHEN: I have a system to follow up on assignments, I'm on time (or early) for class, I get 90s and above on my homework, and it's turned in on time.

GOAL #1:

I'LL KNOW I'VE SUCCEEDED WHEN:

GOAL #2:

JUNIOR AND SENIOR YEAR CHECKLIST

I'LL KNOW I'VE SUCCEEDED WHEN:

GOAL #3:

I'LL KNOW I'VE SUCCEEDED WHEN:

Remember your goals must be SMART. So, now let's break them down into simple action steps to ensure success. How will you reach each goal? What are three simple things you can do?

SIMPLE ACTION STEPS TO ACCOMPLISH GOAL #1:

SIMPLE ACTION STEPS TO ACCOMPLISH GOAL #2:

SIMPLE ACTION STEPS TO ACCOMPLISH GOAL #3:

IN CASE YOU NEED MORE WRITING SPACE:

THINGS TO WORK ON PRIOR TO JUNIOR YEAR:

☑ Get involved in extracurricular activities.

☑ Open a savings account.

☑ Build your credentials and keep track of any awards, community service achievements, and anything else you participate in.

☑ Create a résumé. Google high school student résumé examples.

☑ Create a new professional email address for scholarship applications.

☑ Begin researching and preparing for the SAT/ACT. Look up spring testing dates and where to get free study materials.

☑ Create a study plan that works for your learning style and academic situation. A two-month study plan may consist of 6-7 hours a week (more time if you're not the best test taker).

☑ Stay on track with classes. Stay connected with your counselor to make sure you're enrolled in the right classes you need to graduate.

☑ Write down ten career options and try to shadow someone in these career fields (don't limit yourself).

☑ Volunteer and complete community service hours.

☑ You can start your college search.

JUNIOR AND SENIOR YEAR CHECKLIST

☑ Make sure your social media doesn't give a bad impression of who you are. Be smart with what you post!

THINGS TO WORK ON FALL OF JUNIOR YEAR:

☑ Start using the calendar on your phone to stay organized.

☑ Start studying for SAT/ACT and any AP exams as soon as the school year begins.

☑ Ask your counselor about the PSAT.

☑ Stay on top of ALL assignments and attendance and keep your GPA up!

☑ Make a list of things you may want to study in college.

☑ Create a LinkedIn profile and keep your résumé updated with things you're doing during the year. School stuff does count (awards and involvements)!

☑ Research other educational options: vocational-technical schools, career colleges, two-year or four-year colleges, and military options. This is just so you're aware of your options.

☑ From your list of things, you want to study, jot down five careers/jobs that align with them and research which college majors you will need for those jobs. Lastly, research how much each job pays.

☑ Ask your counselor if any college fairs are coming up that you can attend. Google some as well and attend them!

☑ Begin planning campus visits for local colleges and ask your parents to take you on college tours over spring break.

☑ Add the SAT, ACT, and AP exam dates to your phone's calendar.

THINGS TO WORK ON FALL OF JUNIOR YEAR:

☑ Always stay active, be involved in extracurricular activities, and volunteer 1-2 weekends a month (food pantries are good and feeding the homeless).

☑ Find opportunities to position yourself as a leader (this is a good look on your résumé).

☑ Building relationships with your teachers and other professional adults. You will need letters of recommendation, so get cool with adults who can help you.

☑ Read and find educational content about your major on YouTube. Watch videos related to what you want to do in life as well.

☑ Learn something new and practice being disciplined.

☑ Create a daily routine schedule and stick to this and your goals.

☑ Look for scholarships that let you apply as a junior and apply to as many as possible!

JUNIOR AND SENIOR YEAR CHECKLIST

THINGS TO WORK ON SPRING OF JUNIOR YEAR:

☑ Keep up the extracurricular activities and study for ACT/SAT, then take the ACT or SAT.

☑ Review college/major information and narrow down your college choices. If you haven't already, plan some college visits for spring break, summer, or over a long weekend. You can always start with colleges near you, even if you don't plan to attend them just to get a feel BUT also aim to visit schools that you're interested in!

☑ Find out what's required to get in from the school list you created.

☑ Research types of financial aid and keep applying for scholarships.

☑ Start thinking about your senior schedule and speak with your counselor to ensure you're on track with the credits needed to graduate. See if there are any AP classes or dual enrollment opportunities available.

THINGS TO WORK ON SUMMER OF SENIOR YEAR:

☑ Please be sure to look for scholarships and apply.

☑ Consider getting a job to gain experience, build your résumé, and save money for college.

☑ Ask people about their college experiences. Ask specifically what they wish they knew or would have done differently.

☑ Find out how much your top 5 schools cost for the year.

☑ Start drafting your college application essays. Have someone you know who graduated college read and share feedback with you.

☑ Keep applying for scholarships. Remember, the more you knock out this year and over the summer, the more you can relax senior year.

SENIOR YEAR CHECKLIST

THINGS TO WORK ON FALL OF SENIOR YEAR:

☑ Make sure everything from the junior year checklist is completed.

☑ Always stay active and involved in extracurricular activities, volunteering, and finding opportunities to position yourself as a leader (this is a good look on your résumé).

☑ Keep your résumé updated.

☑ Know your ACT/SAT scores and the requirements from the schools on your list. If you plan to retake them, ensure you are studying 2-3 months before retesting day. Know the next testing dates as well.

☑ Stay on track with classes: Make sure your schedule meets graduation standards and doesn't have unnecessary classes. Talk with your counselor. See if there are AP, IB, CLEP, or dual enrollment courses you can take to get college credit this year.

JUNIOR AND SENIOR YEAR CHECKLIST

☑ Revisit the career option/college activity you started junior year. Make updates as needed to your school and major choices. Be sure to research the starting pay based on the selected degree types and majors. Make a spreadsheet of this info to help you stay organized.

☑ Try to shadow people doing these jobs to learn more about them.

☑ Keep applying for scholarships. You can write one solid letter and keep tweaking it for what you're applying to (depending on the essay question).

☑ Work on and revise your college essay letter (this is your personal statement).

☑ Make sure your social media isn't giving a bad impression that doesn't REALLY reflect who you are. Be smart about your digital fingerprint.

☑ Start using your phone's calendar to stay organized (if you haven't).

☑ Use that spreadsheet you created (with the career options), and on another tab, list all the schools you are applying to, with the admissions, financial aid, and scholarship deadlines.

THINGS TO WORK ON FALL OF SENIOR YEAR:

☑ Being organized and staying focused will save your life this year!

☑ **YOU HAVEN'T GRADUATED YET!** So, stay on course. Colleges will look at what you did senior year, too.

☑ Keep your LinkedIn profile and résumé updated with things you're doing during the year. Remember, school stuff counts!

☑ Get 2-3 people to write recommendation letters for you. Have them ready to submit with college applications. Don't ask people at the last minute. Give them a 1-2 week notice before you need it. Keep all deadlines on your calendar!

☑ Ask your counselor if there are any upcoming college fairs to attend for scholarship assistance and for college application fee waivers. You should be eligible for a waiver if you qualify for free or reduced lunch. Use the common app when you can to apply for schools at once.

☑ If you are applying for early admission and have everything (application, essay, recommendation letters, test scores, transcripts), go for it and keep track of whom you applied to and the status of your applications in your Google spreadsheet. You can visit my website if you need one: www.rahkalshelton.com/collegebound

☑ If you are not applying for early admission, start gathering all your items (application, essay, recommendation letters, test scores, transcripts), create folders for each school, and add the documents to keep organized.

☑ Keep track of every school you are applying to and requirements in your Google spreadsheet. Add all application deadline dates to your calendar so you don't feel rushed.

JUNIOR AND SENIOR YEAR CHECKLIST

☑ Squeeze in any last-minute campus visits (ask about virtual options if you can't travel far) but know that most application deadlines are just before spring break.

☑ Fill out FAFSA (financial aid) forms as early as possible; these usually open the first week of October.

☑ Keep volunteering and participating in activities to stay productive and build your résumé. Update your personal statement to reflect any new things you've done.

☑ Start applying to colleges if you have everything, including your test scores. If you are already applying, check the status of the schools you applied to.

☑ Consider working part-time over winter break to gain experience and save money after graduation.

☑ You should always be applying for scholarships, even over the break. Winter break is a great time to knock out many small things. Consider dedicating a day to scholarship applications. For example, you spend 3-5 hours applying for scholarships every Saturday. Trust me, free money is always worth these 3-5 hours. You can substitute your social media time scrolling and apply for money!

THINGS TO WORK ON SPRING OF SENIOR YEAR:

☑ Keep saving money and applying for scholarship money!

☑ Don't stress! Enjoy this time, too! If you stay organized and on top of things, your stress will be very minimal!

☑ Check the mailbox and email for college notifications. Most decisions go out by March and April.

☑ Keep your grades UP!

☑ Jot down how much each college will cost and how much financial aid and money you need to attend. This should motivate you to apply for scholarships!

☑ If you are put on a waitlist, don't be discouraged. You will know if you can get in before graduation.

☑ Prepare and study hard for any last testing: AP, IB, CLEP, and finals.

☑ Have some fun spring break, but also keep applying for scholarships.

☑ Choose which school you will attend from your acceptance letters. Consider the cost, distance, and major to help you decide. More about this ahead!

☑ Don't pick schools just because your friends are going. Think about YOUR future and what makes more sense for your pockets and life. Do not just base this decision on tangible things, popularity, or what your parents want. Talk with them about the plan and get their support, but this is the life that only YOU will need to live.

☑ **KEEP APPLYING FOR SCHOLARSHIPS. THERE IS STILL TIME TO RECEIVE MONEY!**

THINGS TO WORK ON SUMMER BEFORE COLLEGE:

☑ Work a job and save. Keep applying for scholarships.

☑ Prepare for orientation, research the school you're attending, learn more about the city (if you are moving), and keep saving.

☑ Make a list of what you will need for college to ask your loved ones for support.

☑ Have parents throw you a trunk party.

CHAPTER THREE
COLLEGE, UNIVERSITIES, TRADES, AND ENTREPRENEURSHIP

Over the last twenty years, I've watched the transition from high school to the workforce evolve tremendously. In my parents' day, for many Blacks (a step below the middle class whose families weren't college-educated), getting a job at the post office or local warehouse or entering the military after high school was the thing to do. Going to work just after turning 18 provided many with a sense of responsibility and security, and it didn't require too much. Things are different now, and there are far more options and alternatives.

In this chapter, we'll review quite a bit of vocabulary and the differences in college, entrepreneurship, and workforce options for life after graduation. I want to ensure you understand what's out there and that you can follow what I'm saying. If I share something you don't understand at any point, please use context clues and do a quick Google search. I can't tell you how important it is to fully comprehend everything you read, always! Reading comprehension will be your biggest asset in college.

Before I go any further, just in case you didn't know, "middle class" refers to people who are not quite rich but also not poor. These people are in between and usually have professionals and business people in their families. And a vocation or trade refers to a type of job or job skill.

High schools back in the day had trades like home economics, auto mechanics, and cosmetology. If you took up a trade in school, you were likely more prepared or minimally exposed to different career opportunities before graduating. At the same time, in many urban Black communities in the decade I was born (the '80s), teen pregnancy, drugs (from the crack era), and dropping out of school were also common. That said, things could have gone either way. You could have gotten caught up with trouble or stayed in school and benefited from vocational classes, garnering exposure to different career options.

Fast-forward twenty years later. Vocations in high school and students immediately going to work after graduation slowly became a thing of the past. More millennials (like myself) were eager and curious about postsecondary education, even if our parents dropped out.

When I say postsecondary education, I am talking about college. Secondary education is your schooling between elementary and high school. Postsecondary is after graduation.

Unlike my parents' generation, we had shows like *The Cosby Show* and *A Different World*, movies like *School Daze*, and the immersive celebration of HBCUs as marketing exposure. Although many HBCUs were established just after the Civil War in 1865 through the early 1900s, once they hit TV and became more popularized in our homes via movies and music, getting an acceptance letter for a Black girl, like the white girls did on TV, wasn't too far-fetched. School and being educated became waaay cooler.

At least, this was my reality. I did not come from a family of academics. Many people I knew were just trying to stay alive or get out of the hood, and some of us saw college as a ticket to a better life. Now, being over sixteen years removed from my undergraduate days, I can't fully say that college was, in fact, my ticket to a better life. Before I tell you why, let me break down a little vocabulary so you'll better understand a few things. Some of the terminologies you'll see are also mentioned in subsequent chapters.

DIFFERENCE BETWEEN COLLEGES, COLLEGE TYPES AND UNIVERSITIES

(important vocabulary)

College refers to school after high school, a community college, a technical (trade) school, or a liberal arts college.

University is a larger institution that offers both undergrad and grad degrees (master's and bachelor's degrees).

Community college is a college that serves a surrounding community, offering certificates and a two-year degree or associate's degree. These are also known as junior colleges.

College vs. University. These differ in program offering and degree type. Universities offer bachelor's and master's degrees. A college may only offer an associate's degree.

HBCU stands for Historically Black Colleges and Universities. These institutions were established before the Civil Rights Act of 1964 and even as far back as the mid-1800s. They were founded as a safe space for Black students to access education and attend college without being harassed, hated, discriminated against, or murdered.

PWI stands for Private White Institution. These are universities with 50 percent or more white students enrolled or historically white schools.

Ivy League. This originally was a sports term referring to a specific group of prestigious PWI schools. Consisting of Harvard, Yale, Princeton, Columbia, Brown, Dartmouth, University of Pennsylvania, and Cornell University. Now, it refers to predominately prestigious PWI schools.

Undergrad is short for undergraduate. It's the time spent in college after high school. Undergrad refers to a four-year degree.

Grad is short for grad school or graduate school. It's additional school after undergrad. Typically, it takes one to two years to finish.

Associate's is short for an associate's degree. A type of degree you get in two years from a community college or dual-enrollment high school program.

Dual enrollment is a program that allows high school students to take college classes while in school so they'll graduate with college credits and sometimes an associate's degree.

Bachelor's is the degree you get after four to five years at a university or college. This is your undergrad degree.

Master's is the degree you get in grad school after your bachelor's degree. This is your grad degree.

Gen-Ed is short for general education, which are classes you take freshman year of college before getting into your major or field of study. For example, they are your basic college-level math, history, and English classes.

Major. This is your focus area while in school. It's your field of study in a degree program in college.

Minor. This is your secondary focus area while in school. This is optional but available if you want to study two things.

Field. This is a bit broader than a major. For example, your field could be communications, but your major may be journalism, marketing, radio/TV, and film. These are each in the field of communications but with different majors.

Program. This is the same as your major. You may hear people ask what program you are in, and you'll say your major.

School. This is where your major classes are taken. You may hear someone say, "I am in the school of communications," meaning only communications students take major courses there.

Trade/Vocation. A vocation is a trade or a profession in a specialized area or field. For example, esthetician, cosmetologist, electrician, plumber, etc. This is kind of like a skill you pick up. You don't necessarily have to attend a four-year university or college to get a trade.

Professor. This is your teacher at the college level.

The Workforce. This refers to going straight to work after high school.

Entrepreneurship refers to someone who organizes and runs a business, working for themselves and earning their own income.

Early Admissions refers to receiving an acceptance or decision letter from a college before the usual notification date.

FAFSA stands for Free Application for Federal Student Aid. You fill out this form to determine your eligibility for financial aid from the government.

EFC stands for expected family contribution. This is a number you get after doing FAFSA that helps to determine your award amount.

Full-Time Student is a student taking twelve credit hours or more a semester.

Part-Time Student is a student taking six to eleven credit hours a semester.

UNIVERSITIES

Universities are larger institutions that can be public or private, offering both undergraduate and graduate degrees. Many universities are known for lit and exciting campus experiences and cultures. Universities usually have large campuses and a variety of program options.

Public universities usually enroll thousands of students, and private universities are smaller and more selective with whom they accept. For example, Texas Southern University, a public HBCU, may enroll over 10,000 students. The University of Georgia, another public university, may enroll over 40,000 students. In contrast, Princeton University, a highly regarded

PWI and Ivy League school, only serves 8,000 students. Families who can afford private education for their children will typically pay for it. This is for many reasons.

Universities also typically spend more time on research, and their campuses may offer elaborate labs and large facilities to conduct research better. These institutions get money from the state. Lastly, the selection of professors at more prominent schools is typically the best of the best.

Pros of Universities
- More programs/degrees to choose from that may better line up with your skills, passions, and career desires.
- More diversified communities can help you meet/connect with people from different cultures and countries.
- You can get a bachelor's and master's at the same place if you decide to get two degrees.
- Getting a bachelor's vs. an associate's can help you potentially earn more money.
- Classes are typically led by highly reputable professors, providing a rich, dynamic learning experience.
- Earning a bachelor's or graduate degree can open you to more lucrative professional opportunities.

Cons of Universities
- It can be very expensive and cause you to get into debt if you take out too many loans to try to pay for school.
- Some universities may feel too large, making connecting with your professors and getting to know people harder.
- The classes you want may fill up faster than you can register for, and you can end up with a crappy schedule.
- Larger institutions can be intimidating, making you feel lost, like a number, or isolated due to the number of students on campus.

COLLEGES

Many people use the word "college" when describing school after high school, as if all colleges functioned like universities. I think we say this because it's easier, to sum up postsecondary education with the word college. Hence, the title of this book College Bound, but technically, a college, as mentioned in the previous vocabulary, denotes community, vocational, liberal arts, or technical learning facilities. For example, if you wanted to learn about doing hair or dentistry, you could attend a dental or cosmetology college.

Most actual colleges only offer programs that award associate's degrees, licenses, or certificates. However, some colleges do offer bachelor's degrees. For example, Spelman College in Atlanta is a private, historically Black, women's liberal arts college. Spelman was founded in 1881 as the Atlanta Baptist Female Seminary but received its collegiate charter in 1924. Spelman is America's second oldest private historically Black liberal arts college for women.

We will talk more about HBCUs in a moment. But for now, you've probably noticed the difference between a university and a college. Colleges can feel more intimate and quainter because they are less overwhelming and usually have a smaller student count and fewer program and degree offerings than universities.

Many colleges in the U.S. are private and are not awarded money from the state like many universities. Without state money, most colleges are less dedicated to research, allowing more time for instructors and the institution to focus on you, the student, and your program. Colleges may have religious affiliations as well.

Here's a quick way to spot the differences in college types. For example, a liberal arts college like Spelman may take a broad approach to education, emphasizing the importance of studying various academic subjects vs. a specific thing. From an exposure perspective, learning a little bit of everything makes sense. However, as previously mentioned, other colleges have programs for specific areas, such as cosmetology, phlebotomy, massage therapy, or engineering. These are considered vocational/technical colleges. These vocational or technical colleges are usually for a small and select group of students with specific interests in a single field. If you want to be a massage therapist, cosmetologist, or engineer, you won't attend a liberal arts school. Make sense?

While liberal arts colleges don't necessarily prepare you for specific jobs, they equip you with transferable skills that can help you across various fields. We'll talk more about transferable skills in a later chapter. Liberal arts colleges are great for those who want to focus more broadly on the arts, sciences, humanities, and social sciences.

Some students go away to college just for the experience without truly understanding what's available. Therefore, knowing the difference in college types—technical/vocational, liberal arts, and community colleges is essential and can save you lots of time and money. As you consider your college options and the reason you want to attend, be honest with yourself, for you, not your parents. This is a big decision, and it's your life to live, no one else's. If you plan to attend college just to party, hang out with friends, or find/discover yourself, this isn't the smartest plan. Not only is it too costly, but it's a waste of your precious time and talents. **But** if you have tens of thousands of dollars to blow on having a good time, go for it, do you, but it's still not smart.

Then, there are community colleges known for affordability and convenience, depending on your situation and lifestyle. These are smaller in class size and offer more individualized encounters. Community colleges are less specialized than tech and vocational colleges but offer more options. Attending a community college can be a great way to complete all gen-eds (general education) classes for a low cost if you plan to attend a university later.

Most schools have transfer programs, but some larger universities do not accept community college credits, especially from different states. So, you'll want to make sure the university will accept the credits if you decide to take gen-eds at a community college or transfer to a university. Verify this before transferring.

Community colleges can be a great idea to save money while having the flexibility of working while in school if you choose to. Community colleges can also aid in obtaining your degree faster while providing more intimate access to your professors. In recent years, I've witnessed many community colleges upgraded with state-of-the-art facilities. So don't rule this option out. Your local community college may have everything you're looking for from a program and cost perspective. We will dive into saving strategies in another chapter.

And hopefully, by the end of this book, you'll be a bit clearer, sure, and have a better idea of this college process. If you're still unsure, you can reread this before graduation and consider enrolling in a community college just to get started while you create a future plan.

Lastly, tech or vocational colleges are trade schools offering two-year degrees in specific areas. The cost is also lower here, and the class sizes are cozy. The cool thing about trade or tech schools is that you likely won't need to take gen-ed classes because you'll get to dive straight into your career of choice. Going this route may be the best if you know what you want to do.

Pros of Colleges
- More affordable cost, especially community colleges.
- Focus more on teaching vs. researching, unlike major universities.
- Smaller classes allow you to know your classmates and professor, getting hands-on attention if needed.
- A great way to knock out those gen-eds (core classes) is at a community college.
- Tech/vocation schools allow you to dive right into studies aligning with your desired career.

Cons of College
- Limited study options, programs, and majors. Less variety than in a university.
- Not as diversified as larger schools, and depending on your location, it may feel like you're back in high school.
- Smaller colleges, especially liberal arts schools, may not offer as much financial aid.
- Limited resources and access to better equipment and facilities.
- If you plan on transferring, not all big universities will accept your community college credits.

HBCUS

Ah, the joy, liberation, and celebration of culture experienced at Historically Black Colleges and Universities, also known as HBCUs. What can I say? As a proud graduate of Texas Southern University, I'm a little biased. However, as I discuss this section from my experience and many of the experiences of fellow HBCU alum closest to me, I'm challenged with the desire to give it to you as straight as possible. Yet, I am limited in words to gracefully and adequately articulate the full expression of attending an HBCU.

First, let's dive into a little history. Historically Black Colleges and Universities were established after the Civil War in 1861-1865 to help Black people obtain the basic human right of full access to education. Before the Civil War (please google Civil War if you haven't heard of it), Black people were not allowed to be educated, primarily in the South and many places in the North. Consequently, there were only a few Black schools around. Therefore, groups of good-hearted people with money who wanted to help Blacks succeed and get educated began founding Black colleges and universities. Not only was it important for Blacks to have an education, but also to be educated in safe spaces where we weren't harassed, discriminated against, ostracized, or even murdered.

These institutions gave us a sense of pride, inclusivity, and importance. Prominent Black leaders like Vice President Kamala Harris as of 2023, Oprah Winfrey, Dr. Martin Luther King Jr., the first Black U.S. Supreme Court Justice Thurgood Marshall, award-winning filmmaker Spike Lee, and NFL Hall of Famer and TV host Michael Strahan (who attended my university) are all products of HBCUs, and the list goes on and on.

I must admit attending an HBCU provides a deep sense of safety, security, and family. Many of the campus cultures are unmatched, and although predominantly Black, still diversified with shades, perspectives, and cultures within cultures of Black students. Becoming a successful alum of an HBCU provides you with an opportunity to dispel myths and stereotypical beliefs of Blacks not being academically competitive or prepared for the real world.

As a successful alum of an HBCU, every day, you'll have the opportunity to deposit a dosage of Black Girl Magic into American culture, breaking down walls, kicking in doors, cracking glass ceilings, and becoming your ancestors' wildest dream. Most importantly, you can become a new standard committed to empowering and reaching for others as you continue to climb.

HBCUs offer exciting and empowering opportunities to be on campuses where you're celebrated vs. tolerated. However, when I mentioned the part about reaching for others as you climb, this segues me into some of the challenges associated with HBCUs that could impact your course to graduation. My goal as an auntie, big sister, coach, or mentor figure is to ensure that you are knowledgeable and prepared as much as possible for whatever institution you choose.

If this is your choice, I'll share some challenges that HBCUs face, followed by helpful pointers for thriving at HBCUs. One thing for sure: if you choose to attend an HBCU and graduate, you'll gain an abundance of life skills, including resilience, grit, self-advocacy, and responsibility, to say the least.

CHALLENGES THAT HBCUS FACE

Limited funding can negatively impact the university's ability to provide better resources, the latest technology, and better buildings and infrastructure. Limited funding affects the quantity and variety of program offerings, financial aid, and higher-quality leadership. All this is important to improve education, career preparedness, and exposure.

Accreditation is important for every institution as it helps determine if an institution meets or exceeds minimum quality standards. Some HBCUs have accreditation issues due to low graduation rates, low pass rates for licensure exams, or low postgrad employment rates.

Endowments are another source of funding that varies. Endowments may include funds from private corporations and government agencies, but primarily from individual donors, former students, and alumni who want to give back and help other students.

Quality staffing is important to ensure administrative dealings are proactively handled. Without high-quality staff and solid leadership, problems with the quality of academic programming, logistics, and administrative needs arise. This all translates into students' frustration with advisors, getting individualized help with housing, financial aid, enrollment, and class professors.

While these challenges exist at many HBCUs, this may not be the case for all. It is gravely important to do your research. Learn more about the administration and whether the school has received any recent funding, endowments, or partnerships. You want to review the types of programs offered, find out what student services are available and set up a tour to see the campus. You and your parents must ask the right questions, network, and build relationships with internal staff. This helps tremendously!

If you decide to attend an HBCU, you'll need to go focused and committed to staying on your academics. Taking initiative and being proactive about internships, studying, reading ahead, and taking advantage of every learning opportunity are vital keys to success. Find local alumni chapters for any universities you're considering and connect with them. Alumni chapters are created primarily to provide a community of support for institution graduates while recruiting and supporting others interested in attending.

I am a member of Texas Southern University's Atlanta alumni chapter. My commitment to giving back financially, through books like this and through mentorship, helps to reduce some of the challenges of HBCUs previously mentioned. Through my alumni association, we offer scholarships to local high school students interested in attending Texas Southern. This is the part where I emphasized reaching for others as you climb. HBCU alumni donations and participation are critical to the success of all HBCUs.

For example, I thrived at my HBCU, and I believe it was for a few reasons, including having advocates to help me navigate the culture, campus politics, and the financial aid department. I worked hard to receive scholarships and to stand out. I enrolled very determined and adamant about keeping my GPA up, prioritizing my education, and taking college very seriously. Don't get me wrong, I partied and enjoyed campus life A LOT, but I never lost sight of the reason why I was there, which was to graduate. Remaining graduation-focused is most important at any school. You must always remember your why, whether a community college, HBCU, or Ivy League institution.

In closing, the HBCU experience is like none other. For Black girls, the HBCU experience can provide an opportunity to feel safe, seen, heard, and celebrated while learning. You'll be able to build lifelong relationships and friendships while gaining invaluable academic, life, and social skills, preparing you for life beyond the classroom. Just remember to always reach back.

HBCU SURVIVAL CHECKLIST

☑ Develop a prayer life and bring God on campus with you.

☑ Have access to all your personal data: FAFSA logins, your Social Security number, your parent's Social Security numbers, school ID, and payment receipts.

☑ Be sure you know exactly how much aid you qualify for and verify that the school awards accordingly.

☑ Get the names of any administrators who provide important information, and always verify everything you're told with more than one school rep.

☑ Be proactive when handling your business relating to enrollment, classes, health, housing, etc.

☑ Hold people accountable and follow up <u>proactively</u> with all business dealings. Do not wait for people to contact you.

☑ Make friends with someone in financial aid and in your advisor's office who can look out for you and check your info.

☑ Learn as much as you can and take the initiative.

☑ Be on time and be wise with balancing partying and your academics.

☑ Volunteer and serve as well. This looks good on your résumé.

☑ Look for intern opportunities after your sophomore year.

☑ Read your syllabus and ask questions; never wait for your instructors to tell you what to do.

COLLEGE, UNIVERSITIES, TRADES, AND ENTREPRENEURSHIP

☑ Hold your professors accountable for being on time, grading, and office hours. You are paying their salary.

☑ Sit up front and get to know your professors.

☑ Remember, your goal is to graduate.

☑ Avoid dropping too many classes.

☑ Keep your grades up so you don't go on probation.

☑ Take advantage of all the facilities (library, rec, gym, etc.) because you are paying for them.

☑ Do not procrastinate, and demonstrate consistency, discipline, and self-control.

☑ Meet new people and always be open.

☑ Do NOT take out unnecessary loans. We will talk more about this later.

☑ Be choosy and mindful of the company you keep.

☑ Please avoid credit cards!

☑ Always apply for and look for scholarship money.

☑ Be confident and make yourself and your family proud.

☑ Get involved and in the know about what is going on at your school and what's in the news about your school.

PWIS

The U.S. Department of Education defines a PWI as a university that has 50 percent or more enrollment from white students, but it's also used to refer to any university that is deemed historically white. Unlike HBCUs, PWIs usually have robust funding leading to larger program selections, better infrastructure, and high-quality staff and processors. PWIs also lead with endowments 70 percent more than HBCUs. So, there is little to no question about the education quality and access to resources for students on these campuses. However, for many Black girls in predominantly white settings, especially on college campuses, acceptance, inclusion, safety, mental health, and equity become a chief concern.

Just days before I started writing this section, the Supreme Court ruled to overturn affirmative action. Affirmative action has provided countless Blacks and people of color with opportunities to attend top and highly selective universities that they otherwise would not have been able to attend. The simplest way to describe affirmative action is a policy that was implemented to help police underrepresented groups of people (Black and brown people) from being overlooked for opportunities that they're well qualified for and deserve.

When you hear affirmative action, it's mainly referring to education and employment. Affirmative action helped encourage inclusivity and reduce selective schools and employers from using race as a factor in admissions. On college campuses, Black students are already underrepresented at selective and highly selective schools and even at the popular universities in the state (flagship universities).

What does this mean for you if you are interested in a university? It could mean a few things, and the impact will vary from school to school. However, it could mean higher enrollment at HBCUs, little to no recruitment of talented Blacks for selective schools (PWIs) across the country, a lack of diversity on campuses, a decline in Black and brown students enrolling in med schools, law schools, etc. Also, the same is true for work environments and places of employment.

We'll be able to get a better gauge of what this means in the coming months and years. For now, I wanted to mention this as a great segue to address some issues facing Black girls on predominantly white campuses.

Unlike our white counterparts, campus location and passing through certain neighborhoods at night, especially in less diverse towns, are to be considered. I've read countless Black student reports of stereotypically being harassed in those communities. Students have reported being labeled as underprivileged, ghetto, or unintelligent by professors, classmates, and advisors at these PWIs. False perceptions like these often paint the picture of students as being a joke or needy, causing them to feel a need to prove themselves academically and socially. I've read about the lack of advocacy for Black students and the lack of diversity in the professors, impacting students' ability to connect with their teaching styles. This is extremely important, as every student learns differently.

MSNBC journalist and Black host, Joy Ann Reid recently shared a portion of her story on Instagram. She spoke about being recruited and accepted into Harvard (one of the country's top PWI and Ivy League universities) because of affirmative action. She shared about her first week as a freshman, where her presence was questioned by white students. Joy said she had never had her academics or intelligence questioned until attending Harvard. Students and staff didn't feel she belonged there and only accepted due to affirmative action.

Joy attended Harvard with students whose names were on the buildings because they were third and fourth-generation legacy. This means their parents and grandparents attended Harvard. She says, "Many of the students were less intelligent but had parents who pumped money into the school to ensure their children got in."

Other Black students attending PWIs have reported daily microaggression (these are slick, degrading racial comments and acts), harassment, feelings of insecurity, not being able to connect with students, and a lack of consideration from professors.

In my opinion, primary deterring factors for PWIs boil down to emotional safety and the potential of being denied access or being in environments lacking the respect and need for diversity and inclusivity within the staff and student body.

In closing, my goal isn't to overlook the incredible resources, academic opportunities, and scholastic advantages that a PWI may afford. Nor is it to deter Black students from attending. My desire is to candidly support you with information to make an informed decision.

However, if you decide on a private and selective or highly selective PWI, you'll need to be prepared for potential rejection of admission and some of the adversities mentioned above. Even if you don't identify as Black on your application, factors like the spelling of your name, your zip code, high school, extracurricular activities, and the content of your personal statement letter can point to your ethnicity. I will share more about the admission process shortly.

PWI SURVIVAL CHECKLIST

☑ Everything mentioned in the HBCU survival checklist.

COLLEGE, UNIVERSITIES, TRADES, AND ENTREPRENEURSHIP

☑ Always remember that you are worthy and deserve to be wherever you are. Your authenticity is most helpful, valuable, and necessary over anything else!

☑ Be confident in who you are, and don't fold, dim your light, or pretend to be something you are NOT.

☑ Don't allow people to mispronounce your name, say slick/inappropriate things (about you or in your presence), don't let anyone touch your hair or invade your personal space.

☑ Educate yourself on different forms of microaggressions, tone policing, gaslighting, covert racism, and other discriminatory behaviors.

☑ It's okay to be angry at times (all humans experience this) and to demonstrate emotion but do it intelligently and appropriately.

☑ You don't have to prove yourself or try to be "strong," and it is not your responsibility to represent an entire race.

☑ Connect with people who celebrate you, find your people and get tapped in with any Black student unions and organizations or create one if necessary.

☑ Keep an open mind and heart, extending grace to yourself and others. Always look for learning and teaching opportunities to educate yourself and others.

☑ Uncomfortable communication doesn't have to be super confrontational.

☑ Be direct with your professors and advisors, and don't accept handouts not offered to everyone else.

☑ Learn as much as you can and take initiative.

☑ Be sure to speak up, advocate for yourself, set boundaries, and report any incidents if and when they happen. You train people how to treat you.

☑ Make sure you have an advocate on staff who can help you.

☑ Don't assume every Black person on campus is your friend.

IMPORTANCE OF HAVING A SKILL OR TRADE

If you don't learn or get anything else from this book, please listen to me now; it is so crucial for you to have a trade! When I say trade, I am talking about skills and talents, and there is a difference between the two. However, having either one or both will put you far ahead of the game.

Fortunately, God uniquely created each of us with gifts. These are different from skills and talents. A skill, also known as a trade, is something you learn that can be developed with practice and training, while talents are things, we do naturally that we were born with. Talents can feel similar to gifting. However, your giftings are God-given and align with your purpose.

There is a Scripture, Proverbs 18:16, that tells us that our gifts will make room for us and bring us before important people and decision makers. Think about all the gifted people you know whose gifts have opened doors for them. Beyoncé comes to mind for me. Her singing ability and creativity are undoubtedly God-given gifts, and they have certainly opened doors and placed her on large stages before the world.

While you may not know your gift immediately, it's okay. Don't be too hard on yourself and try to force figuring this out at this age. You can pray and ask God to reveal your gifts, talents, and purpose (if you don't already know them). You can also pay attention to what you're good at and what other people say you're good at. Pay attention to what you care about and what you do easily and naturally. These are good indicators of what God placed inside of you. Remember the exercises in chapter 1? They were intended to challenge you to start thinking about this.

Besides learning about college, this chapter is about understanding the urgency of having a skill. I can't express enough the value and importance of having a skill if you want to make it in life. I know, I know, we live in a day and age where people are getting famous on social media and YouTube for absolutely nothing or something really meaningless. So, you're probably thinking, why do I need a skill when I can go viral?

While this may seem cool at the moment, getting followers and being famous is not a real skill, and it won't be sustainable. I mean, instant "success" hardly ever lasts. You won't even remember these Insta-famous people in a few years, especially if they don't have much to offer after the 30-second reel.

Ladies, your looks and body aren't a sustainable trade/skill either, not even for models or influencers. What if you injured yourself or, Lord forbid, got into an accident that disfigured you? What if social media went away tomorrow? How would you make money to provide for yourself? I hope you understand what I am saying.

Your brain, creativity, hands, perspective, voice, and style can certainly be your moneymaker (skills), and it's essential to cultivate these through practice and learning. For the ladies who think you can get a man to take care of you, that's not sustainable either. What if he leaves or something happens to him?

Think about it like this. Every high-value woman positions herself to be able to independently care for herself. You are a high-value young woman! Granted, your husband can help provide for you IF or when you get married. However, as a high-value single woman, you still need to be able to do something, pulling your own weight and bringing something to the table.

Remember what you bring to the table (your skills) can complement all future partnerships. This is how power partnerships succeed...a smart, resilient, and talented woman who has something to offer pairing with capable, intelligent, supporting, and like-minded others. This applies to business and non-business relationships. When these character traits are combined in partnership, successful magic happens. I'll talk more about partnerships when we dive more into relationships later. For now, let's stay focused on your skills.

Here's something else to consider. College is not only designed to teach free and critical thinking, life readiness, and independence, but more importantly, college is for you to learn something. Hopefully, to garner skills. These skills and disciplines should help prepare you for the workplace and to take care of yourself. You can also consider getting a certification or learning something new that could be a backup skill and a future moneymaker.

You don't want to be 28 years old without a trade/skill, trying to figure out life. Even if it's not something you're really passionate about, having a skill is smart and can always help bring in income. For example, I may be interested in attending school to be a reporter, but I am great at cooking and braiding hair. This could mean that I have two additional skills (cooking and braiding) that I can use to take care of myself while I pursue reporting. Make sense?

We will talk about the importance of entrepreneurship for Black women next, as most people who work for themselves leverage their skills/trades/gifts well enough to start a business with them.

ENTREPRENEURSHIP FOR BLACK GIRLS

Over the last ten years, but mainly since the pandemic, I've seen entrepreneurship become far more popularized and a standard option even out of high school for many young women like yourself. This is especially true if you have natural skills or talents that people will pay you for.

Even if you haven't thought of getting paid for your skills as entrepreneurship, in many ways, it is. There are entrepreneurs as young as 3 and 7 years old getting paid to play with toys, post videos, review content, or play video games. While entrepreneurship seemingly appears super easy, it's actually far from easy and requires a lot of discipline, risk-taking, and consistency. This is if you want to scale. When I say scale, I mean grow.

An entrepreneur is defined as a person who organizes and runs a business. These people take on greater financial risk because they usually just go after something they believe in and use their money to make it happen, hoping to make their money back and then some. Back in the day, entrepreneurs used to be called crazy because they were crazy enough to believe in their dreams.

Recently, entrepreneurs have been categorized by different types, including social entrepreneurs, authorpreneurs (like myself), and scalable startups, to name a few. I don't want to get too far in the weeds teaching this, but you can do more research in your free time if you want to learn more. However, I will share some practical entrepreneur types you probably can relate to and consider even as a high school student. Think about a group project that you've recently done in the context below.

- **The creative entrepreneur** is the one with tons of exciting ideas and concepts. They are very creative but may need help staying focused on one project/idea at a time and possibly get bored quickly.

- **The builder entrepreneur** is good at taking ideas and building a business around it. They are good with the money and growing the business. The builder loves motivating others and challenging themselves to grow bigger and make more money.

- **The operator entrepreneur** is an organized person who is great at putting processes in place and good with creating details and ways to make things better. They keep all the goals in mind and help everyone else stay focused.

Consider the one you relate to most, even if you're not considering entrepreneurship. Knowing your style is important to identify the type of help you need in life. You always want to have others around you who are better in the areas you are not. And for Black girls, entrepreneurship is an excellent option to consider in addition to school. Entrepreneurship can equate to financial freedom. Financial freedom means having enough savings, financial investments, and cash to afford the kind of life you want. Doesn't this sound like a dream? Well, it's absolutely possible for you.

Financial freedom is crucial for Black girls because, statistically, we are underpaid in the workplace and in life. This is called the wealth gap. According to the Census Bureau, for every $100 in white family wealth, Black families hold just $5.04. Black families in America earn about $57 for every $100 made by white families.[3] There is a difference between wealth and earnings. In short, wealth is the value of things you own, like money and property. Income or earnings is just the amount you make in a certain period, like your paycheck. So, while Keisha may make $20 an hour at work but rents an apartment, her white coworker, Becky, may own a house and only make $17 an hour. This means Becky has more wealth than Keisha, although she makes less.

Blacks in this country have little to no wealth, and this is because of several factors. I don't have time to get into them, but if you want to learn more, research the wealth gap between whites and Blacks and why it exists. You can also read a copy of my other book, *Woosah: A Survival Guide for Women of Color Working in Corporate*. As a high schooler, this book may be a little advanced at your age, but it's definitely a great read later before finishing college.

I'll say this again: Entrepreneurship can be a strategy for gaining financial freedom. It's also a good alternative if you decide college isn't for you. Furthermore, getting a college degree doesn't guarantee making lots of money. You may

---

[3] E. Badger, "Whites Have Huge Wealth Edge Over Blacks (but Don't Know It)," 2017, The New York Times, https://www.nytimes.com/interactive/2017/09/18/upshot/black-white-wealth-gap-perceptions.html.

actually leave school with way more debt than you entered with. And there's a chance you may not find a job in your field even with a degree or be paid accurately. I'm not trying to depress you but to empower you to learn as much as possible, so you are prepared for the real world. This is why this book is so important to read and keep as a reference to go back whenever you need it.

Maybe you don't want to run a business or be an entrepreneur, but that's fine, too. You can still consider creating another income stream even while in school. Remember I talked about getting paid for your skills? Seriously, having more income while in college can help you save, reduce stress, help others, or cover tuition.

Suppose you're considering entrepreneurship instead of college. In that case, you will still need to know some business basics unless you have a dedicated mentor to help you. Think about those entrepreneur types shared earlier. You can't only be the creator entrepreneur because who's going to make the sales, create the systems, and manage everything?

Attending workshops or taking business classes, even if not getting a full degree, is smart, or consider getting a certification before entering full entrepreneurship. Gaining business knowledge classes will teach you to price yourself, get organized, and even talk to people demonstrating good customer service. Great customer and client service is everything for an entrepreneur or business owner because you want customers to keep returning, especially if the service and experience are good.

For example, I've met a few makeup artists off of Instagram who were talented and skilled in doing makeup. Still, they were rude, didn't know how to communicate, and were disorganized. I am a tipper who loves to tip and appreciate great service. But with their disorganization and poor customer service, do you think I tipped or will ever return? NO! Imagine if these artists had more business and customer service training; how much better they could be.

Just because you have talent does not make you a business owner. If you are serious about entrepreneurship, get out there, shadow and learn from established entrepreneurs, take some classes, even virtually, and learn what you can to improve your offer! Entrepreneurship is a great way to be a free thinker and gain financial freedom.

Consider this: creating an additional income stream besides your job's check will help you not only thrive in life but also help to reduce the stress associated with responsibilities, car notes, doctor bills, and everything else with its hand out asking for money. Adulting can be tricky, and thinking about ways to make extra money now can help you in the future. When you gain new skills and trades, you are better positioned to earn more income, which can help boost your quality of life.

Don't get me wrong, money can't buy happiness or joy, but it can get some of your time back and reduce pressure. More money **can** help to make life more enjoyable. Think about it like this. What if you had a side hustle of braiding hair in college, and the extra money you made went toward your books or savings account? You could also use the extra money to go home on the weekends and spend quality time with your loved ones.

Do you see how that works? Consider the 24-year-old you who has a degree and working full time on a job or for yourself because you started an online T-shirt business using your graphic design skills, and the money from that business allows you to save, invest, and take a vacation four times a year. Awesome, right?

I want to close this chapter with two things. First, I want to acknowledge where I left off earlier, discussing my mindset leaving high school. I thought college was my ticket out of the hood. Looking back sixteen years after undergrad, college was an incredible experience that taught me much about life. I grew into womanhood in college and gained skills for a successful career in broadcast media and coaching. However, I can't fully say that college was, in fact, my ticket to a better life. After graduating high school, I was underprepared and unaware of all the options I had access to. I wish I had a book like this then, which is why I am writing this for you now.

Also, I alluded to something a few paragraphs earlier. College didn't guarantee the money I thought I would make. It didn't prepare me for the adversities I would face as a Black woman in the workforce, including being underestimated, discriminated against, and underpaid with significant college debt.

Earlier, I talked about my observation of how trades and vocations seemingly have shifted from schools. While many schools encourage STEM and STEAM at earlier ages to expose youth to various skills, these programs are still offered within a college readiness context. Many schools in the U.S. focus on preparing students for college as if college is the end-all and for everyone. I can't say that it is.

I believe the more students are discouraged from exploring trades/vocations and pushed into pursuing college, the more students remain boxed in. I am all for students knowing their options and being able to explore college, universities, side hustles, entrepreneurship, and working a bit. Knowing what options exist is important.

However, with schools pushing for students to test, test, test, and prepare for college vs. exploring and strategizing, students are becoming less in tune with their innate gifts, skills, and talents, thus producing college graduates with lots of book smarts and limited practical experience or street smarts.

COLLEGE, UNIVERSITIES, TRADES, AND ENTREPRENEURSHIP

Furthermore, this college prep notion industry pushes many students, mainly Black and brown students, into deeper debt if they don't have scholarships, college funds, or means to pay for school. To worsen matters, many Black women later become gravely disappointed to learn that college isn't always a ticket out but often a setup for financial problems with more profound consequences. That was my experience. After graduation, I dug myself into a financial hole because I didn't know what options existed, nor did I have help along my journey.

Higher education (colleges and universities) is a very lucrative service industry. They make millions of dollars from students without a guarantee that students will earn money back from their four-year investment. Here are some stats about Blacks and college debt according to an article on bankrate.com.[4]

While you may not really understand the stats on the next page, they are unsettling and something to consider as you and your parents think through how you plan to pay for college.

---

[4] Heidi Rivera and edited by Helen Wilbers, "Student loan debt statistics by race," Bankrate, November 07, 2022, https://www.bankrate.com/loans/student-loans/student-loan-debt-statistics-by-race/.

- Black students take out most student loan debt for a bachelor's degree.

- Black borrowers have an average student loan balance of $30,000.

- Ninety percent of Black students take out student loans for college, compared to 66 percent of white students.

- After graduating, Black students hold almost twice as much student debt as their white peers, largely due to differences in interest accrual and graduate school borrowing.

- After graduating from college, 17 percent of Black students are behind on their student loans, compared to 9 percent of white students.

- Out of women undergraduate borrowers, the average Black woman has the most student debt, averaging a little under $42,000 one year after graduation.

- Almost 71 percent of Black undergraduates are Pell Grant recipients, meaning they come from low-income households.

Traditional college paths aren't for everyone, but they can be worthwhile when done right (smart and strategically). Depending on what you want to do with your career, college may also be necessary, especially if you're interested in being a doctor, lawyer, or public servant. I hope I can help you create a smart plan that will set you up for future success.

Lastly, entering the workforce means getting a job right after high school. This is a viable option, but you may hit a stumbling block when it comes time to earn more money or be promoted if you don't have a degree (associate's or bachelor's), skill, or certification. This isn't always the case, especially for those with in-demand quality skills, but it is certainly something to keep on your radar.

There are things you can do to expand your learning and résumé. If you decide to skip college and go to work first, depending on your field and the job, consider getting a certification, intentionally learning more, or taking some classes. These actions help to demonstrate your commitment to growing and sharpening your skills. Whatever you do, do not get complacent and comfortable with a $22-$23-an-hour job. You were created to earn and do more significant things in life, and remember, you don't have to do it alone.

CHAPTER FOUR

SCHOOL SELECTIONS, AND THE APPLICATION PROCESS

In previous chapters, we learned what a major is and the difference between colleges and universities. In this chapter, we'll dive deeper into how to choose your major, how to change it, and the importance of having one. We will also talk about minors as they relate to majors and some other good stuff. I hope you're still doing okay and keeping up with me. I totally understand that this is a lot of information, but prayerfully, it is very helpful, easy to follow, and inspiring.

Little sis, this is truly one of the most exciting times of your life. Even if it doesn't feel like it, it can be! I don't know what you're personally going through, but I want to encourage you to shift your focus to all the wonderful opportunities that ARE at your fingertips. You are embarking on an AWESOME life and an exhilarating journey that you get to decide! How cool is that?! And when you make smart decisions (intentional and strategic ones), there is no way you can go wrong.

But, if you feel you have gone wrong, going wrong always produces an opportunity to learn more about yourself and what to do next time. While God ultimately controls our lives, He loves and trusts us enough to let us co-create with Him. That said, you have more power and control over what happens next in your life than anybody else, including your parents.

During my time in the classroom and as a mentor, I sadly came across parents who didn't want and wouldn't let their sons or daughters go away to college or study in a specific field they were passionate about. Some parents even refused to help their children with the application process. This always broke my heart!

Listen to me. While most parents truly mean well, as a young woman creating your own future, you've got to be careful not to allow your parents' fears to stop your potential. I've met mothers who didn't want their daughters to go away to school because they wanted them to stay home to help around the house or with little siblings. Some mothers didn't even believe their daughters were smart enough for college but masked their lack of support behind saying they didn't want to see them fail. Other mothers didn't want their daughters to attend college because they thought their daughters would be smarter than them or leave them forever.

I don't know your relationship with your mother, father, or guardian, but I hope they encourage you to shoot for the stars and not only encourage you but also tangibly help you get there. On the flip side, some of the fear your parents may feel about you starting college is warranted. As your parents, they want to protect you and be accessible if you need help. Then again, if your parents are attentive, they can see your struggles and weaknesses and help steer you in a more sensible direction.

For example, if you're not good with kids, lack patience, and have a bad temper, but you're interested in studying to be a pediatrician, your parents may advise that this isn't smart. Attentive and supportive parents can recognize flaws and encourage you in ways to help reduce those flaws. These types of parents are certainly the ones who will best advise you.

Then there are the parents who didn't attend college and just don't know how to help you. They may mean well but just can't give you what they don't know or haven't had. In this instance, don't take it personally. You will still do well because you're resilient and have this book. Moral of story, this decision is yours to make, and it's important, but with wisdom, guidance, and solid support, you will do well. Just ensure you don't allow anyone (including your parents) to box you in, decide with fear, or stifle your growth.

Let's talk about the selection and application process. This process requires some real soul-searching and honest conversations with yourself, God, and your parents. Depending on your relationship with your parents or guardians, you'll need to be very vulnerable, transparent, and open to receive their guidance but also able to spot their limitations.

For the conversation with God, He always enjoys being included in your life's decisions and longs to support you. Ask Him to reveal what He wants you to study, what He created you for, and to show you which path to take. Be open and look for coincidences, random things lining up, and maybe any dreams. Listen to your mentors and teachers who are looking out for you. Perhaps God will speak through them. I call these coincidences the God dots. Remember those connect-the-dots coloring sheets and how every dot connected created a picture? That's kind of what our lives are like. Think about other God dots when little things work out and line up. That's all Him looking out for you.

Little sis, it's not the universe doing this but the Creator of the universe who is in charge. God! And He's always speaking, especially about the big matters in our lives. For the times when you can't identify what He's saying, take a leap of faith and go for it, trusting your gut. God can't steer a parked car, meaning as you get moving, He can lead and guide you, like a GPS system...even if you need to be rerouted, you're in good hands.

That last conversation is one with yourself. You'll need to be really honest about what you want or what you think you want. It's okay if you don't fully know this YET. But be real about your strengths and weaknesses, passions, and things you don't like. Go back to the questions in chapter one to help guide you. Are you ready to get into the selection process and everything else? Let's go!

HOW TO CHOOSE YOUR SCHOOL AND MAJOR

Your major is important because it sets the tone and serves as a guiding light for your college experience. It's the foundation for your studies and degree, while your minor isn't your major. The minor can either complement your major or allow you to learn something else. For the first year in college, you likely will not be taking major classes yet.

Remember we talked about gen-eds? Yep, these will come first. You will need to knock out those gen-eds and then declare your major and select a minor if you choose. Please know that a third or half of your classes in college will be in your major or related to it if you didn't select a tech/vocational school.

When selecting a major, most students pick majors aligning with their passions and minors that will complement their major. For example, if you wanted to be a sports reporter, your major may be communications with a minor in journalism. With every degree plan, students will need to select a major. Having a minor is optional.

Some students decide to have double or dual majors. A dual major lets you earn two credentials in distinct fields, and a double major allows you to study two areas. However, you'll still receive only one degree. Both options can assist with a wider array of career options. This can be expensive, producing additional work and more time to graduate.

College credits are packaged as something called per credit hour. Per credit hour is the amount you will pay per credit hour. Usually, when students are enrolled in certain credit hours, this can be a flat fee. For example, a biology class may consist of four hours and cost $200 per credit hour, meaning that one class will run you about $800. This is why I mentioned that double majors can be more expensive because you're taking more credits. Every graduation major and plan will have a unique amount of credits needed to obtain that degree. More on this breakdown in chapter 7.

What if you don't want to major in anything or are uncertain which major to select?

You can consider being a general studies student, which means you don't have one specific focus. Your major then is general studies. I believe general study majors can be a colossal waste of time, money, and focus. However, you can choose to explore a few things if you're undecided and then pick something closely aligned with what you're good at or interested in. Remember, college is expensive and better leveraged when attending strategically. You will hear me repeatedly say strategic or strategy in this book because it's so important. Having a strategy is having a plan.

What if I have a change of heart? Can I change my major?

Yes! You can always change your major but remember that whatever classes you've taken towards your previous major may not translate into the new one. This could mean you lose money, energy, and time. Imagine going to college thinking you want to be a sports reporter, and you start taking communications classes, but over the summer, you get a job at a hospital that you love! Next thing you know, you decide you now want to be a doctor and change your major. This means you now have communications classes that may not fit into a biology/medical major. While you probably learned a lot in communications, you don't need them now as a doctor. This is why I mentioned doing some soul-searching and figuring out what you may really like upfront.

When thinking about your major, you want to consider how much it will cost you, how much money you want to make, and if it's a major you can see yourself working a job in.

I presume you're still in high school, so this means you still have a little time to explore, but keep this on your radar for when the time comes to select your major. If you're out of high school and already in college, you can use some of those previous classes as a minor or as electives. I'll get into electives and credit hours in a bit.

For now, think about this. Most careers and jobs today are geared towards service, creativity, or making money. This isn't to say the three can't coexist. However, if you can get them to coexist, making money from your creativity or serving others, then you've hit a serious sweet spot.

Here's another kicker. Most people don't land jobs in their majors or intended fields outside of STEM options. If they do, they don't always stay. I say this to say while your major is super important to guide you to graduation (especially for a

STEM field), there is some flexibility, and if selected strategically and thoughtfully, you'll have the upper hand to make whatever you choose work for you.

Until you get there, think about whether you want a job that helps others or allows you to be creative, or are you just interested in making money? Depending on your career choice, how you're wired, and what you are passionate about, you may care more about art or serving others vs. making money. Some of you may care more about making money than art or helping others. This is something to consider as you select your major or career field. Depending on your choice, it may or may not permit you to make the money you want.

Speaking of money, let me clear the record. Little sis, there is nothing wrong with wanting to make money! As Black women, making money is sometimes frowned upon or viewed through a poverty lens. Making money does not mean you think you're better than anyone. It means you've worked hard to earn it. Please don't let anyone make you feel embarrassed about wanting to make money or earning nice things. As you know, money is important for several reasons, including sustaining and caring for our families or ourselves, paying off/avoiding debt, living more comfortably, saving, investing, or helping others.

However, knowing that money can't bring you true happiness is super important, as well as knowing that the love for money is the root of all evil. This means that when all you care about is money, the control that money has over you can get you in lots of trouble and damage relationships. So, if you desire more money, just make sure your heart is in the right place and that you'll use your money for good and to help others.

I challenge you to think briefly about how important money is to you. Noted is a sample list of career fields that make lots of money vs. those that don't. You will notice that many higher-paying jobs align mostly with STEM options (science, technology, engineering, and math) vs. STEAM. The A was added to include the arts. Take a look below, and we'll dive deeper into the process of selecting a major and school. I'll provide you with some tools to help you fully research and decide what may be right for you.

LOWER PAYING MAJORS/CAREER FIELDS
Data From Indeed and Glassdoor[5]

DESIGN AND APPLIED ARTS MAJOR
Career Options:
- Fashion Designers
- Game Designers
- Graphic Designers
- Illustrators
- Interior Designers

AVERAGE YEARLY SALARY $49,290

SOCIAL WORK MAJOR
Career Options:
- DCFS Worker
- Family/School Counselors
- Mental Health
- Healthcare

AVERAGE YEARLY SALARY $56,750

---

[5] Paula Sumner, "10 of the Lowest-Paying Majors (Plus How To Increase Salary)," *indeed*, July 27, 2023, https://www.indeed.com/career-advice/finding-a-job/lowest-paying-majors.

HOSPITALITY & TOURISM MAJOR
Career Options:
- Travel agencies (flight attendants, airlines, tour guides)
- Restaurants
- Hotels
- Event Planners
- Customer Service & Sales

AVERAGE YEARLY SALARY $24,470

PSYCHOLOGY MAJOR
Career Options:
- Clinical
- Counseling
- School
- Industrial-organizational

AVERAGE YEARLY SALARY $78,200 (with advanced degree)

THEOLOGY & RELIGION MAJOR
Career Options:
- Pastors
- Biblical Studies
- Preachers
- Missionary/missionary studies

AVERAGE YEARLY SALARY $31,630

ELEMENTARY EDUCATION/HEALTH & PE MAJOR
Career Options:
- Teaching students
- Provide a welcoming and engaging classroom
- Provide instruction materials
- Teaching gym and coaching students

AVERAGE YEARLY SALARY $59,670

HIGHER PAYING MAJORS/CAREER FIELDS

SCIENCE/CHEMISTRY/MED/BIOLOGY MAJOR
The numbers below reflect average base yearly salaries.

Career Options:
- Cardiologist
$185,036
- Anesthesiologist
$359,207
- Surgeon
$298,537
- Psychiatrist
$271,705
- Physician
$176,568
- General Practitioner
$133,017
- Optometrist
$355,696 ($171 per hour)
- Veterinarian
$128,597
- Pediatrician
$161,611

BIOLOGY/PHARMACEUTICAL SCIENCE MAJOR
The numbers below reflect average base yearly salaries.

Career Options:
- Orthodontist
$271,196
- Dentist
$220,518
- Periodontist
$298,537
- Obstetrician
$192,8917
- Pediatric Dentists
$256,389
- Pharmacist
$164,230
- Pharmacy Manager
$121,439
- Pharmacy Tech/Assistant
$121,439

MATH/COMPUTER SCIENCE & ENGINEERING MAJOR
The numbers below reflect average base yearly salaries.

Career Options:

- Quantitative Analyst $137,781
- Director of Information Security $146,923
- Software Architect $135,724
- Software Engineering $156,949
- Aeronautical Engineer $104,405
- System Engineers $103,838
- Engineer $100,184

BUSINESS/ FINANCIAL / MATH MAJOR
The numbers below reflect average base yearly salaries.

- Economist $109,902
- Mathematician $109,014
- Director of Operations $98,293
- Accounting Manager $112,778
- Project Manager $86,544
- Sales Manager $82,486

WHAT TO CONSIDER WHEN DECIDING YOUR NEXT

WHAT'S MOST IMPORTANT TO YOU?

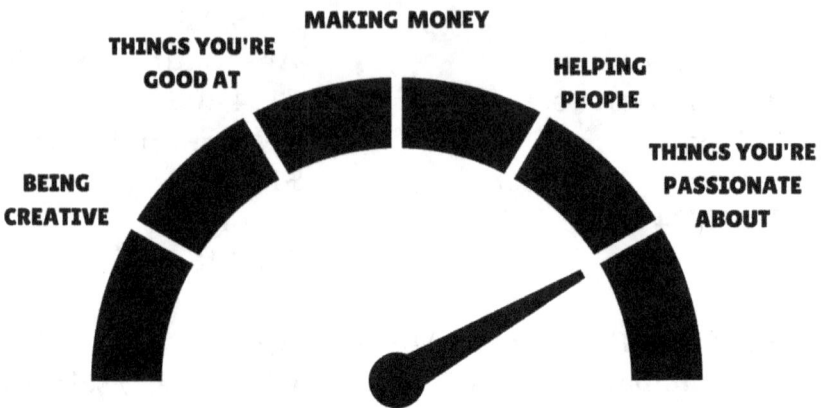

- Are you leaning towards college or working after graduation?

- If the school offers the degree type (associate's, bachelor's, master's) and major/program you're interested in.

- If you plan to be a full-time or part-time student.

- Knowing if you are interested in public, private, PWIs, selective, or an HBCU.

- If the school is affordable for your financial situation and not too expensive.

- If you need to take out loans.

- What types of scholarships, grants, and financial aid does the school offer?

- How hard is it to get in? Will your GPA/transcript/test score meet the requirements?

- Are you interested in a big school, big city, or small school, small city? Will you be a minority?

- What is the culture like? Will your new campus home fit/feel good?

- How are the instructors, graduation rate, and career placement office?

- What activities/opportunities are offered there?

- Does the location work for you? Do you want to live on or off campus?

- Does school make sense for your lifestyle or the one you want to create?

HELPFUL TIPS FOR SELECTING A MAJOR

1. Decide what's more important to you. What are your biggest priorities? Is your focus to be creative, working on your passions and skill areas? Are your priorities to be able to help others, or is it to make money? These may overlap, but start with thinking about what's important to you. Ask yourself what is most important for me on a scale of 1-10?

2. Identify what you're interested in and good at. Also, consider taking a personality quiz to help uncover your strengths. Google Myers-Briggs Type Indicator, which is a good personality test. Also, google recommended majors that align with your interests and skills.

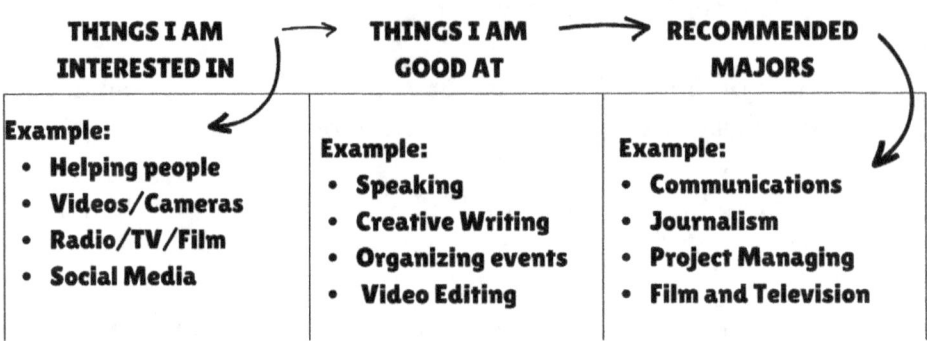

YOUR TURN:

Things I'm interested in:

Things I'm good at:

Recommended Majors:

3. Find out your earning potential (the money you can make) and which majors will help you land higher-paying jobs.

4. Find out how rigorous and challenging the major may be. You will need to be real with yourself here. You know you very well, so if you're unwilling to work and focus on a challenging major, don't waste your time or money. Pick something that better suits your skills and talents.

5. Speak with family and friends who went to college about their process and how they selected their major.

6. Speak with your school advisor and research different types of majors.

7. Do not allow your parents' or anyone else's fears, insecurities, or plans for your life to discourage you from following your gut and passion.

8. If you're still undecided, do a little exploring. You typically don't have to pick a major until your sophomore year, anyway, but be intentional while you explore, learn, and research as many major options as you can.

HERE ARE SOME PRIMARY MAJOR CATEGORIES

Arts and Humanities
- Majors in art and humanities usually take a multidisciplinary or combined approach to education. These programs combine the study of languages, literature, art, music, philosophy, and religion.

Social Sciences
- Programs in social sciences focus on how individuals behave within society, how society works, and the relationship between them.

Health and Medicine
- Majors in health and medicine focus on the study, research, and knowledge of health principles and how to apply that knowledge to prevent, diagnose, and care for humans and animals.

Public and Social Services
- Programs in public and social services prepare students to study, manage, and provide public programs and services. Areas of focus include law/legal studies, public administration, social services, protective services, and more.

Trades and Personal Services
- Trades and Personal Services programs prepare students for careers that require manual, mechanical, or technical skill sets. These programs are highly specialized and combine traditional classroom learning with hands-on experience.

Business
- Programs in business involve teaching the skills and operations of the business industry. Business majors cover a variety of areas including accounting, entrepreneurship, finance, marketing, human resources, economics, and more.

Interdisciplinary Studies
- Programs in the interdisciplinary areas of study combine two or more programs together through a common theme and allow students to specialize their degree to their many interests.

Science, Technology, Engineering, and Math
- Programs in STEM include majors in four disciplines — Science, Technology, Engineering, and Math. The skills needed for each discipline overlap and studies in these fields provide students with a multidisciplinary skill set.

10 THINGS BLACK GIRLS SHOULD CONSIDER WHEN SELECTING A COLLEGE

THE DEGREE OFFERINGS AND AVAILABLE MAJORS/PROGRAMS

THE LOCATION (THINK SAFETY, COMFORT, ACCESSIBILITY, AND HAVING THE SUPPORT)

THE COST

THE SIZE OF THE SCHOOL

MAKE SURE THE SCHOOL IS ACCREDITED AND LEGIT

PRESTIGE, REPUTATION, AND ACADEMIC QUALITY

AVAILABLE RESOURCES, INCLUDING CAREER READINESS SUPPORT

CAMPUS LIFE/ENVIRONMENT, STUDENT BODY, AND EXTRACURRICULARS

GRADUATION RATES AND EDUCATION STATS

THE SCHOOL'S HISTORY, INCLUDING THE QUALITY/DIVERSITY OF STAFF AND PROFESSORS. HBCUS ARE NOT EXEMPTED

SCHOOL FINDER AND MAJOR SELECTION RESEARCH ACTIVITY

1. Select a major from the primary major category page or from what you Googled and wrote down (based on your interest/skills) earlier. If you already know what you want to major in, write that down.

I am interested in majoring in:

My backup major options are (these are other areas you're skilled in):

2. Research and list other possible names under which your major may be listed.

For example:
Major: Broadcast Communications
Desired Job: Sports Reporter

This major may also be listed as Journalism, Media Communications, or Broadcast Television. The options may be listed differently depending on the college or university and the programs they offer. I don't want you to think a school doesn't offer something just because it doesn't show up how you searched for it. This activity will help you explore different major options in case it's under a different name. Make sense? You can also do a Google search for "What major do I need if I want to work in this (fill in the blank) profession."

3. After you've identified your program/major, we can start looking for schools that offer it. Create a list of schools that offer the programs you are looking for. I recommend listing about 12-15 and then dwindling that list down so you're not too overwhelmed. You can select less or as many as you like.

4. Of your list, at least 3-5 of those schools should be local (in the city, neighboring states, and/or community colleges no more than 2 hours away). The purpose of this is to help reduce costs. The other ten or so schools can be wherever. Be sure to dream big and add whatever schools you like, especially if you have the grades for it. Have fun and see what's out there. Your list will continue to dwindle as you get closer to graduation. Below is a sample to help you keep things in one place. You can create your own, adding more columns or taking some away. This is just an idea to get you started and organized as you create your list. My student clients and I use Google Docs. You can visit my website, www.rahkalshelton.com/collegebound, for a complimentary electronic copy. Have fun and make this list your own.

Create a spreadsheet capturing the information below.

- School
- Application Deadline/Cost
- Tuition
- Requirements (GPA, ACT/SAT)
- Location
- Major /Degree

SCHOOL SELECTIONS, AND THE APPLICATION PROCESS

Get creative and make the spreadsheet your own. For example, your columns can look like this:

SCHOOL	TUITION	APPLICATION DEADLINE	APPLICATION COST
Georgia State University	In-state: $10,268 Out-of-state: $29,306	Early: October 15th Regular: March 15th	$60

REQUIREMENTS	MAJOR /DEGREE	GPA/ACT/SAT
TRANSCRIPTS, GPA, TEST SCORES, LETTERS OF RECOMMENDATION, FAFSA DOCS, ID/DL/PASSPORT, PERSONAL STATEMENT	BACHELORS OF ARTS MAJOR #1: TELECOMMUNICATIONS MAJOR #2: MASS COMMUNICATIONS	GPA: 3.4 OR HIGHER DOESN'T NEED TEST SCORES. GPA: 3.3 AND UNDER SAT – READING: 24, MATH: 22 TOTAL SCORE: 1090 ACT – ENGLISH: 17, MATH: 17, TOTAL COMPOSITE: 19

5. Research and create a list of 5-10 jobs you can do based on your selected majors. When researching these jobs, list the starting salaries as well. Use the names you've researched in #2 to find these jobs.

For example: Major: Broadcast Communications
Desired Job: Sports Reporter
Other jobs I can apply to with a communications degree:

JOBS AND SALARIES FOR COMMUNICATIONS DEGREE

Social Media Strategist
Social media strategists in 2023 earned a median salary of $56,329, according to Salary.com.

Journalist
According to the U.S. Bureau of Labor Statistics, reporters, correspondents, and broadcast news analysts made a median salary of $48,370 in 2021.

Public Relations Specialist
According to the U.S. Bureau of Labor Statistics, public relations specialists earned a median salary of $62,800 in 2021.

Marketing Manager
Marketing managers earned a median salary of $133,380 in 2021, and the field is expected to grow by 10% through 2031, faster than most other professions, according to the U.S. Bureau of Labor Statistics.

THE COLLEGE APPLICATION PROCESS

We've covered so much information in this chapter, and I hope you're more informed and confident as you begin this part of your journey. Please do not overwhelm yourself. I really want you to have a blast and know that everything you need (for the most part) is in this book, with your counselor, or one question away.

Be sure you find someone who you trust and who's knowledgeable to help you implement and understand what you're learning. Be sure to ask them questions about their college process or even the times they've applied to different jobs. You can also check out videos on YouTube regarding other people's college application experiences.

You want to ensure you put your best foot forward in the application process. This is the prime time to sell yourself and speak to all the values, skills, and experience you can add to whatever school you decide. If you're reading this, the application process starts now, like right now. It starts with keeping your grades up, getting organized, getting involved, learning as much as possible, volunteering, reading, taking AP or dual enrollment, and doing everything in the checklist I provided early on.

Many colleges offer early admissions options. This can be a good idea if you already know what college you want to apply to, assuming you've also done your research, calculated the cost, and visited. However, a downside to early admissions is when those other letters come in later. There is a possibility that another school may offer you more money, thus making it difficult to compare your other offers if you've already accepted or committed.

Early admissions can be either an early decision plan or early action plan. In the early decision plan, you are essentially committing to the school that accepts you and lets you in early.

With the early action, you can decline an offer if you choose. If you decide on early admissions, be sure you know what you are signing up for.

At this point in your life, your grades are your tickets/keys to success, as they will either open doors for you or make it more challenging to get into locked doors. In short, the application process consists of the following:

- ☑ Deciding if you will be a part-time or full-time student (part-time is a student taking under 12 hours a semester).

- ☑ Keeping your GPA up, getting involved, and taking the ACT or SAT (you can always retest or take both if you want to submit a higher score). Consider dual enrollment.

- ☑ Identifying your school and program.

- ☑ Find out the deadlines and what's required to apply (usually done in the fall of your senior year or earlier).

- ☑ Writing a personal statement.

- ☑ Collecting recommendations. Even if not required, please submit one anyway. This helps you stand out! Ask a mentor, teacher, supervisor, auntie, or someone who can speak to your character and work ethic. Don't wait until the last minute to ask them. Give them two weeks' notice.

- ☑ Apply for scholarships and complete the FAFSA. Do this as soon as it opens, usually October, but opening in December in 2023. More about this in the next chapter.

SCHOOL SELECTIONS, AND THE APPLICATION PROCESS

☑ Begin filling out the application and paying for application fees (some schools will offer fee waivers. Look for these, always!).

☑ Use the common app or whatever your counselor advises.

☑ Make sure your transcripts are submitted directly to the school.

☑ Sit back and wait for the award and acceptance letters to come in.

CHAPTER FIVE
PAYING FOR COLLEGE, SIDE HUSTLES, AND FINANCIAL FREEDOM TIPS

Hey girl, hey! We've made it to the money chapter, which is certainly one of those chapters to bookmark, explore with your parents, and keep coming back to. In this chapter, my goal is to discuss strategies regarding paying for college, saving, making money in college, and how to graduate with as little debt as possible!

In previous chapters, I challenged you to consider what field you want to enter and your degree and college type. These are all important factors to help determine the amount of money you'll need for college and can help gauge your earning potential after college. We also discussed thinking through and weighing the value of passion/service work vs. more lucrative work.

Remember, colleges and universities are profitable service industries themselves. They provide students with education, and we pay for them. They make millions of dollars from students without a guarantee that students will earn money back from their four-year investment. For Black women, studies show that we are among the most college-educated demographic in the U.S. and simultaneously underpaid and in the most student loan debt. Isn't that something? If you are anything like I was at your age, you're probably wondering why.

Although I mentioned the wealth gap earlier, allow me to paint a brief picture of just how this gap exists. I want to equip you with more context because knowledge is power. Then, I'll get into the financial aid breakdown and other strategies.

WHY ARE BLACK PEOPLE BEHIND FINANCIALLY?
The wealth gap illustration

Let's say 24-year-old Becky inherited a paid-off house worth $300,000, which she promptly moved into (similar to the example I gave earlier). She also had a 529 college savings plan established for her at birth that was continuously growing. Her parents paid for college, so she had no student loan debt. Her parents were in a position to do these things because their parents had wealth, setting them up for success. Becky then landed a job with a salary of $55,000 per year.

Meanwhile, Keisha, also 24 years old, earns $70,000 per year but rents a condo and owes a whopping $100,000 in student loans after earning a master's degree. In an effort to be more competitive, earn more money, and increase her chances of landing a good job, she returned to school for her master's. This additional degree is what pushed her college debt up to six figures. Keisha's hardworking parents couldn't leave her a home, start a college savings plan, or pay off her college debt.

Although hardworking, Keisha's great-grandparents were slaves, and her grandparents were raised during the Jim Crow Era (please google this era). Consequently, they were subject to many obstacles, including being denied home mortgage loans and higher paying jobs, all because they were Black, thus making it difficult to set her parents up for greater success.

If we are speaking solely about income, Keisha makes more money than Becky. However, when we look at Becky's and Keisha's wealth, it's evident that Keisha has more debt than Becky. What's the bottom line? Becky has a higher net worth than Keisha. This is the case for many Black Americans. The wealth gap that many Black people experience stems from our country's historical injustices. Historical injustices like slavery, segregation, gentrification, a lack of access, and discriminatory practices regarding business loans, home loans, and other funding resources contribute to the lack of wealth in minority communities.

If Keisha's grandparents hadn't been discriminated against, were able to purchase a home, and received equal pay for their hard work, they would have been better positioned to leave assets for her parents. Keisha's parents would have been able to start a college savings plan and provide Keisha with a home as well.

Much of the adversities we face as Black women mainly boil down to receiving equal opportunities. While whites can accumulate wealth and pass it on to subsequent generations (hence the valuable property Becky inherited), the children of Black and brown families usually have to start from scratch. This type of imbalance keeps Keisha financially lagging, even though she draws a larger salary than Becky. And guess what? Neither woman is at fault. They are simply playing the cards they have been dealt. And as a Black woman, it's not only important to play the hand that you're dealt, but confidently, with wisdom as well.

God isn't surprised by what we have or where we are. Ultimately, He is our provider—not the government, employer, or anyone else. Those are just resources, but God is our source, and He's in control.

I've witnessed these gaps in my own life. I'm only 39, and my grandfather was a sharecropper who grew up in Jim Crow. He had to drop out of third grade to help his father work the land. My grandfather hardly had anything tangible to give my mother. He did pass down some intangibles, such as integrity and hard work. These are all wonderful, but character doesn't pay the bills. My mother didn't have any knowledge about finances or wealth. At times, she didn't even have the means to pay her rent, let alone save for college, and she worked hard daily, often two to three jobs.

This may not be your story. Maybe your parents have been saving for you and are financially sound. If so, this is so wonderful! However, understanding gaps and systemic issues facing Blacks in this country is vital. Also, learning about another's hardships helps produce empathy, even when something isn't your story. Empathy is important to keep the world a better place.

Do these systemic issues define you? Absolutely not! Is anyone coming to save you? No ma'am. But because you are reading this book, I know you are the type of woman who wants to do something great with your life. And you have a chance to do and go further than your parents and grandparents did. With knowledge, hard work, discipline, and commitment, you can!

HOW TO PAY FOR COLLEGE AND WHAT FAFSA IS

College is paid for primarily through financial aid (FAFSA), personal loans, scholarships, or directly out of pocket if you can afford to pay directly. FAFSA stands for Free Application for Federal Student Aid. You fill out this form to determine your eligibility for financial aid from the government. Most students apply for FAFSA, which usually opens on October 1 but is opening in December in 2023 and ends on June 30, unless they do not need assistance paying for college.

FAFSA applications require your information and your parents' unless you are considered an independent student. Independent students are not claimed on anyone's taxes and are financially independent from their parents or guardians. The U.S. Department of Education also defines anyone as an independent student if they are:

- At least 24 years old
- Married
- A graduate student
- A professional student
- A veteran
- A serving member of the armed forces
- An orphan
- A ward of the court
- An emancipated minor
- An individual with legal dependents other than their spouse
- An individual who's homeless or at risk of becoming homeless

Financial aid is dispersed on a need-based and semester schedule. Need base means more assistance is available to lower-income families. The formula for deciding awards considers the income and assets of students' parents. This information is used to create what is called an EFC. The EFC is your expected family contribution. The higher your EFC, the lower the amount of aid you will be rewarded. Colleges will also consider your EFC to help determine what they can offer you.

It is very important to begin working on FAFSA as soon as it opens to increase your chances of getting the maximum aid amount. Most grants and scholarships are first come, first served. If you wait too late, you can certainly miss out, and keep in mind that you are competing with everyone in the country applying for aid, including graduate students. FAFSA looks at investments, savings, checking account balances, and basically all your family's business (you and your parents).

If you have siblings in college or going around the same time as you, having your parents complete FAFSA for both of you can help reduce your EFC, which can help you get more money. If your parents are unmarried or file tax returns separately, be sure to use the information of the parent who makes the lesser income. Please note, if you use this parent's information, they will need to claim you on their taxes, so you are not giving out false information to the government. You can learn more directly at www.studentaid.gov.

After applying for FAFSA, the school you will attend will award your funds. Be sure to stay on top of communication with your financial aid advisor to ensure your documents are properly processed and the school has your information. Your part-time or full-time status also factors in the amount of aid you receive. Full-time students are eligible for more assistance than part-time students. Financial Aid is defined in four major buckets:

FINANCIAL AID TYPES
Grants
These are forms of financial aid that are completely free and don't have to be paid back (unless you leave a school and you own money or there is a stipulation to receiving the grant and you don't hold up your end of the bargain).
Different federal grant options:

- Pell Grants
- Federal Supplemental Educational Opportunity Grants
- Teacher Education Assistance for College and Higher Education (TEACH) Grants

Need-Based Scholarship
Most scholarships are from nonprofit and private organizations that want to help students pay for college or career schools.
Scholarships are also free money, usually based on your academic merit, talents, unique circumstances, or a particular area of study.

Top scholarship search sites:
- Scholarships.com
- Fastweb
- College Board
- Going Merry
- ScholarshipOwl
- Bold.org
- Cappex
- Scholly
- CareerOneStop
- Niche
- Peterson's

Work-Study Jobs
Work-Study is a program option that allows you to work on campus part-time, earning money to pay for college.
Most work-study jobs will pay the current minimum wage, but you can earn more depending on your work and the skills required for the position.

Your work-study amount is based on:

- When you apply
- Level of financial need
- School's funding level

Loans
A loan is money you borrow and must pay back with interest. It's the interest and taking out unnecessary loans that usually cause debt.

The primary loan types are:
- Subsidized Loans. These are for eligible undergraduate students helping cover college or tech school costs. The Department of Education pays the interest on these loans while you are in school.

- Unsubsidized Loans are for eligible undergraduate, graduate, and professional students. Eligibility for this one is not based on financial need. You (the borrower) are responsible for paying the interest on these loans while in school.

- Direct PLUS or Parent PLUS loans are available for graduate or professional students and the parents of dependent undergraduate students to help pay for education expenses. Eligibility is not based on financial need; a credit check is required. If you are an undergrad student and your parents are denied this loan, you may be eligible for something else. However, these loans can damage your parents' credit if you cannot repay them immediately. You likely won't be able to pay them back immediately. You can also decline this loan.

- Direct Consolidation Loans allow you to combine all your eligible federal student loans into a single loan with a single loan servicer. I did this, and most people do.

If you apply for financial aid, you may be offered loans as part of your school's financial aid offer. When you receive a student loan, you borrow money to attend a college or career school. You must repay the loan as well as the interest that accrues. It is important to understand your repayment options so you can successfully repay your loan.[6]

SCHOLARSHIP MONEY

Hundreds of thousands of FREE dollars go unclaimed yearly due to students not applying for scholarships. One of the most effective ways to pay for school by reducing or avoiding student loan debt is through scholarships. Scholarships are financial support awards for students to help them pay for an undergrad or grad degree. Scholarships can be based on academic achievement or other criteria that may include financial need for the purpose of schooling. There are various types of scholarships, the most common being merit-based and need-based.

Merit-Based Scholarship
These are granted based on your academic or extracurricular achievements, such as grades, test scores, athletic or artistic accomplishments, or community service. These scholarships reward and encourage excellence and usually require students to meet specific eligibility criteria for consideration. If you have a renewable scholarship, you must continue to meet specific requirements.

---

[6] "Types of Financial Aid: Loans, Grants, and Work-Study Programs," FederalStudentAid, https://studentaid.gov/understand-aid/types.

Need-Based Scholarship
These are granted according to your financial need. Factors such as family income, assets, and other circumstances impacting your ability to pay for college are considered to assess your eligibility decision. After completing the FAFSA, a need-based scholarship may be set up to help cover tuition, fees, room and board, and other college expenses for students who may not have the financial means to pay for college independently.

Scholarships differ from loans because they do not need to be paid back. Scholarships can come as a one-time check, and other scholarships are renewable, providing students with money each semester or the entire school year. While mentoring and tutoring at different high schools, I've witnessed students refuse to apply for scholarships because they didn't feel like writing "all those essays." Seriously, I've heard students flat-out say, "I don't feel like writing." I can't tell you how disappointing and lazy this is!

At the same time, I get it (as much as I can). Writing additional essays on top of your regular workload can feel like a lot. But it's the things we often don't feel like doing that we have to. Think about it like this. If I want to remain healthy and in shape, I still have to get up and go to the gym after working all day. Your parents still come home to cook and provide for you after a long workday. And you still have to do your chores after a long school day. In life, we will constantly be faced with things that bring great rewards, yet they are things we don't want to do.

This is the same for scholarships. IF you really want a solid shot at paying for college with other people's money and graduating debt-free, you'll need to apply for scholarships. And if you do it right (strategically and thoughtfully), this can be easy, especially if you get organized. You can consider writing one to three REALLY good essays and tweak them to fit each scholarship you apply to. Getting on a schedule of applying as frequently as possible also helps your chances of getting free money.

There is a lovely young woman who recently graduated with my niece from Westlake High School in Atlanta. She was accepted to over fifty colleges and universities and earned over $1.3 million in scholarship money (please Google her). While my niece didn't earn a million dollars in scholarship money, she was awarded enough to cover tuition and fees until she graduates.

For my niece's classmate, her secret to earning over $1.3 million in scholarship money was tackling the process by starting small, strategically, and thoughtfully. She kept her GPA up and spent a few hours each day applying to scholarships and schools. She began this process in her sophomore year and had a full ride by the time she became a senior. "Student loans are something that I do not want. So, this is kind of a gift, both to myself and to my parents," she was quoted as saying.

What if I helped you create a plan and system for scholarship applications? Will you be willing to put in the work and gift you and your parents with free college tuition? I hope so! The first thing is to work on your GPA starting now.

TIPS FOR BOOSTING YOUR GPA
- Do not miss class or assignments.
- Stay in great communication with your teachers.
- Ask for extra credit and retakes when available.
- Study hard and frequently.
- Be proactive vs. reactive.
- Be intentional about your GPA.
- Avoid distractions.

BEST PRACTICES WHEN APPLYING FOR SCHOLARSHIPS

- Create a new professional email address that you will use strictly for scholarship applications.
- Create accounts online for various scholarship search sites (use your new email address).
- Create a schedule of when and how often you will apply.
- Put that schedule in your cell phone calendar and follow through.
- Create a spreadsheet in Google Docs to help you organize (see the scholarship organizer example).
- See if the college or university that you are looking at offers scholarships.
- See if you qualify for any state-based scholarships.

EXTRA SCHOLARSHIP FINDERS

Beware of scholarship scams! You do not have to pay for scholarships or the application process, EVER! Any website asking for money in the scholarship process is a scam! When applying, do not give out your Social Security, bank account number, debit, or credit card information. Look out for scam-looking websites and language that feels like pressure. Below are some additional scholarship locator sites. You can always google more later if you like.

- BrokeScholar.com
- CollegeXpress
- Scholarship America
- Chegg
- CollegeNET

HOW TO ORGANIZE YOUR SCHOLARSHIPS

Create a spreadsheet capturing the information below.

- Scholarship
- Amount
- Deadline
- Requirements
- Any Additional Info

SAMPLE SCHOLARSHIP ORGANIZER

SCHOLARSHIP	AMOUNT	DEADLINE	REQUIREMENTS
COCA-COLA SCHOLARS SCHOLARSHIP	TOTALING UP TO $20,000	OCTOBER 31, 2020, AT 5 P.M. EASTERN.	STUDENTS NEED A 3.0 GPA AND TO FILL OUT AN ONLINE APPLICATION THAT REQUIRES NO ESSAYS, NO RECOMMENDATIONS, AND NO TRANSCRIPTS.

WHAT TO ADD TO YOUR SCHOLARSHIP LETTER

☑ Review the organization's requirements and include everything they ask for.

☑ Make sure you include your contact information.

☑ Open your letter by introducing yourself and sharing why you are applying (real people are reading these letters, so be genuine).

☑ Share all your major accomplishments. This is your time to shine, but don't sound too arrogant. Be humble yet very honest, and highlight all your great work, skills, passions, and any personal milestones you've accomplished.

☑ Make sure you add any unique skills or talents you may have. The more you share, the more the reviewing committee can get to know you.

☑ Share what you want to do in college and as a career and how this opportunity can help you accomplish this.

☑ As you wrap up your letter, you thank them for their time. You can also let them know you are happy to provide referrals and recommendations if needed and they can contact you at anytime.

SCHOLARSHIP APPLICATION LETTER TEMPLATE
(Sample template derived from Indeed.com)

[Full Name]
[Phone number] | [Professional email address] [City, State]

Dear [Include a name or make it to the scholarship review committee],

[Open your letter with a warm introduction, including your grade and whether you're currently earning a degree or if you're a future college student.] [Share something about the organization and how its mission or purpose aligns with you and your goals. Think about why you're applying for the scholarship and highlight how the funding can contribute to your academic and professional success.]

[In the second paragraph, discuss your significant academic or personal accomplishments and how they contributed to your success as a student or your growth as an individual.] [List the unique skills and qualities you possess and discuss how these align with the organization or the scholarship you hope to obtain.]

[Conclude by expressing your passion and interest in your area of study or future career to reaffirm your enthusiasm and what the financial award can mean for your success. Thank the committee for their time and consideration and invite them to contact you if they have questions.] [List your preferred contact methods.]

Best regards,
[Full name]
[Signature]

EASY SIDE HUSTLES WHILE IN COLLEGE

What if you do not get a scholarship before going to college? It's okay; you will keep applying if you are determined enough. You can always apply and receive scholarships up until you graduate college. You can also apply for some while in grad school if you choose to attend. It isn't over if you don't gain any free money before going away. See what your financial aid looks like, and which school offers you more money or a better package.

You can also ask for payment plans and get a job while in school to help pay for college. Although working a full-time job may be less realistic if you plan to be a full-time student, you can consider working part-time or doing side hustles to help pay your college bills. If you choose to attend a university, there may not be a lot of night class options. This means you'll need to attend school during the day and work in the evening.

For freshmen and sophomores, if you can skip working a job that requires a lot of your time, please consider doing so. You want to stay focused on your why, which is school. However, if you decide to get a job, do something most aligned with your school priority and doesn't compete with too much of your time or grades. Here are a couple of side hustle ideas for students. This money can go towards your books, living expenses, food, or whatever you need to help you progress in school.

- Dogsitter
- Babysitter
- Social media manager
- Content producer
- SAT/ACT prep tutor
- High school tutor
- Virtual Assistant
- Graphic designer
- Food delivery
- Hair braider

GRANTS, WORK-STUDY, AND STUDENT LOANS

Personally, I think the rest of these school-funding options are pretty self-explanatory. Your FAFSA application will be sent to your school, determining what you qualify for regarding loans and work-study. However, don't be afraid to visit different departments on campus and inquire if they have any work available for work-study.

Regarding grants, if you're not awarded or offered any after you complete the FAFSA, some can still be obtained through independent searches. Many grants will be listed as scholarships since they operate the same, where you don't have to pay these back. You can create a new spreadsheet to keep track of or simply add them to your scholarship document. Because all the information we'll ever need is right at your fingertips, I trust you'll do a great job searching for grants and scholarships. Below are two additional grant/scholarship websites to get you going.

- Unigo
- Collegescholarships.org

Regarding student loans, if you need them, take them, but take only what you need. I will talk more about this in the following section. However, suppose you were awarded more money than required to cover school. In that case, you can always decline or ask for a lower amount. Your primary goal is to avoid loans and get as many scholarships to fund school as possible. This can be done primarily by ensuring you are exceptional and standing out, getting that GPA up, and maximizing your skills and talents.

Ladies, please never settle for less than average or choose to be mediocre IF you can do more. Even if you see your parents or other adults who you love settling for less, this is not what you want. People who do the bare minimum in life will never reach their full potential or the fullness of who God created them to be. Have you ever heard this quote?

"The graveyard is the richest place on earth, because it is here that you will find all the hopes and dreams that were never fulfilled, the books that were never written, the songs that were never sung, the inventions that were never shared, the cures that were never discovered, all because someone was too afraid to take that first step, keep with the problem, or determined to carry out their dream." —Les Brown.[7]

I would like to add that some of these people just made excuses or chose to be basic. Please hear me out. I'm not saying strive for perfection or be too hard on yourself AT ALL! Perfectionism is just as bad as being basic because it will leave you feeling insecure, exhausted, and chasing something that doesn't exist.

Here's an easy way to tell if you are settling or choosing to be basic. Ask yourself, can I do more (emotionally), or did I give my best? Based on your answer, either go harder and be thorough. But if you pause after checking your emotions, honor this. If you feel emotionally drained, take a moment and start again tomorrow.

There is no limit to starting over. Here's a secret: life is full of starting over moments for those with the courage to start over. If you don't like something, change it. Remember, you have more power than you know.

---

[7] Les Brown, Quotes > Quotable Quote, Good Reads, https://www.goodreads.com/quotes/884712-the-graveyard-is-the-richest-place-on-earth-because-it.

IMPORTANCE OF CREDIT, BUDGETING AND MONEY MANAGEMENT

Refund checks are all I heard about my freshman year's first week on campus. People were too amp to take out student loans (usually way more than needed) to get a refund check. Credit cards were also popular as well because many credit card companies targeted college students, making it easier than ever to get signed up. After all, turning 18 meant you could legally get a credit card. Let me start by telling you what credit cards and student loan refund checks are not:

- Free
- Gifts
- Shopping spree money
- A pass to be irresponsible
- Smart if used irresponsibly
- Helpful for your future emotional health

A refund check is money directly deposited to you by your college. It is the excess money left over from your financial aid award after your tuition and additional fees have been paid. Accepting unnecessary cash from the government is never a good idea, as you will always owe the government until you die. Furthermore, getting credit cards unnecessarily and taking out more money than you need while in school is the fastest way to keep you under extreme debt, making it harder for the future you to be successful.

The bait with credit cards is the 0% introductory APR. They will usually bait you with this to get you to sign up. It seems like, wow, I can access $5,000 and don't have to pay it back right away. But you actually do if you want to keep a healthy credit score and avoid going into debt.

Debt is usually money or something that you owe someone else. Most people in debt usually lack self-control unless there were catastrophic hardships and costly emergencies happening in their lives. The feelings of heaviness produced by financial stress, including owing someone, not having enough, and not knowing how you're going to make it, are the top reasons people feel anxiety, suicidal thoughts, or depression.

When the money ain't right, it doesn't feel good. Not only can debt ruin your life, but it can also negatively impact your credit. You may be young right now, but your future credit will be everything to you. Having good credit can help afford you more opportunities and things in life. Your credit score is used to help you get an apartment, buy a house or car, get insurance, pay utilities, and even some jobs will look at your credit.

Good credit shows that you are responsible, and bad credit displays you as irresponsible. Yes, even if you were only 18 years old, signed up for a credit card and extra student loans, and didn't know better, you will still be held responsible for your choices.

MY COLLEGE DEBT STORY :(

In undergrad, I qualified for a Pell Grant and work-study. Because I was an out-of-state student, my tuition was higher. The Pell Grant and work-study wasn't close to covering my fees, so I also needed loans. I didn't know the importance of applying for scholarships in high school. Shoot, I hardly had help preparing for college; my mother dropped out of the ninth grade, and my big brother dropped out of the tenth grade, so I was the first to embark on this journey, blindsided but determined.

I worked hard, and fortunately, by sophomore year, I was awarded a resident assistant (R.A.) position, which meant my housing was free as long as I worked as a dorm monitor. Resident assistant positions are a form of work-study. Because I was an R.A., my college cost went down that year. However, the school tore down my dorms the following year, leaving me homeless without a place to live or work. I learned this information only a month before the start of the school year. It was awful and hard not knowing if I could afford to return to school because I didn't have a place to stay and had never lived alone.

That summer, I got thick skin and learned to really advocate for myself. I learned more about scholarships and found an apartment and roommate to help save money. I got a job and was offered a scholarship. These helped so much, but I still didn't have enough because living off campus required more living expenses and now rent. Therefore, I needed additional loan money to help me, and I was also helping my mom back home.

Due to the wealth gap that we discussed and many other reasons, it isn't uncommon for many Black and brown students to use student loan money to help with home. As Black women, we are more likely to be in positions where we need to work or help our families while in college.

There, I was over thirteen hours away in Texas. At times, my mother needed my support with my siblings. So, I had to make things work. I used my refund checks and credit cards to live, and on some things, I could have done without, primarily for rent, bills, a car after moving off campus, flights home, etc. I am telling you, I would have done things VERY differently if I had the game given to me like you're getting in this book.

No one warned me about the dangers of accumulating so much debt. By the time I graduated, I was well over $30k in student loan debt and swimming in credit card debt. I ended up moving back home to Chicago and in with a relative to help save money. I worked three part-time jobs, making very little money, and still couldn't afford my bills, including credit card bills. Unfortunately, I didn't have parents who could afford to help me financially. I had to make it work because I didn't have a home to return to.

There I was, an honors graduate from Texas Southern University with a wealth of talent, accolades, professional experience, and an awesome résumé. However, I still couldn't find a full-time job in my field that would pay me my worth. I probably could have landed work in another area, but my degree was in media, and I wanted to chase my dream of being a producer or director.

It was a very challenging time. I remember approaching my twenty-fourth birthday and having a mental breakdown because of the debt and transition into the real world. It had only been one year after I graduated, and I had high expectations.

Adding to my stress, student loan lenders wanted their money already. By the way, if you get either a Direct Subsidized or Direct Unsubsidized Loan, like I mentioned earlier, you only get a six-month grace period before the lenders start hounding you for their money back. As if six months is enough time to find a job, get situated after college, and make payments.

The constant phone calls and emails asking about their money and my credit card debtors became overwhelming. I didn't have the best skills to cope with multiple life and financial stress at the time. Eventually, I ended up enrolling back in school to get another degree. I thought maybe another degree would help me have a better opportunity to get a career job. Looking back, this decision wasn't strategically thought through or the best decision (for me).

Being in grad school, I accrued far more debt and needed loans again to provide for myself after moving out from my relatives. I still worked two part-time jobs in grad school and remained in debt through graduation.

My story eventually turned around incredibly, and God gets all the credit and glory for that blessing! He showed me that He was my provider. He also shifted my purpose and passion for media work to mentoring, coaching, and empowering young women like you. I went to college for one thing, but God had greater plans. This is why I am writing this book: to educate and help you avoid some of the pitfalls I made simply because I didn't know any better.

Remember I mentioned that my grandfather didn't have much to give my mother and how she didn't teach me anything about money or college prep? This isn't uncommon in many Black communities. Most of us haven't had anyone to sit us down and talk to us about money, debt, or credit or someone guiding us. I imagine most of your parents are my age, and many of us had to learn the hard way.

While learning the hard way builds character, being knowledgeable and working smarter saves time and builds stronger generations. This may be your first time learning about the importance of credit right now.

Because this isn't a financial book, I won't dive too deep into how credit is assessed. I trust that if you are interested (and you should be), you will research this on your own. However, I want to provide some base knowledge to highlight the importance of avoiding debt and boosting your credit. Speaking of credit, there is a way to use credit cards and refund checks to your advantage to boost your financial future. For now, check out some credit card statistics by race, according to an article on bankrate.com.

CREDIT AND RACE STATS FROM BANKRATE INSIGHTS:

- Majority-Black and other minority communities have the lowest median credit scores and highest rates of subprime credit scores. Subprime means credit scores of 580-619.

- Among homebuyers, people of color tend to have the lowest credit scores. The average American homebuyer has a credit score of 728, while Black and Hispanic homebuyers have average scores of 677 and 701, respectively.

- Black and Hispanic Americans may have less access to banks, an issue caused by redlining—a discriminatory lending practice that limited access to credit products to consumers living in areas deemed financially risky. The average redlined neighborhood is 32% Black and 30% Hispanic (please google "redlining" to learn more).

- 58% of Black Americans say they have more debt than savings; just 30% of white Americans say the same.[8]

---

[8] Kendall Little and Christopher Murray, edited by Sarah Gage, "Credit card statistics by race and ethnicity," Bankrate, June 07, 2023, https://www.bankrate.com/finance/credit-cards/credit-cards-and-race-statistics/.

As a Black girl preparing to start her professional journey, these numbers are important for a few reasons. A primary reason is to be educated and armed with wisdom to be better, mitigate risk, and help to change these numbers. You and all your classmates are the future! I sincerely believe in preparing the future to be leaders. One of you reading this may be a mentor, doctor, professor, or the boss of my future child, and I want to know that the future is in good hands.

We discussed why avoiding unnecessary debt is important, the stress it can cause, and the value of building good credit. Now, I want to talk about when refunds and credit cards are okay. Refunds stemming from scholarships, grants, or work-study are completely fine and often exciting because you worked hard to receive these funds. Refund checks and credit cards are helpful for you only if you fall into one of these categories.

- You do not have any financial support from family/parents, and you need additional funds to care for your safety and well-being while in school.

- You need additional funds to cover your books, fees, and living expenses necessary to finish college successfully.

Credit cards can be a smart way to build your credit, and refunds can be a smart way to either invest in or support you while in school. The main rule of thumb for credit cards as a college student is to not get anything over $500 or $1,000 and make sure you either only use it in the case of an emergency, or if you use it, pay back EVERYTHING you charged on it each month by the due date and on time.

The smaller the amount you swipe, the less you need to pay back. **I recommend not getting a credit card** if you do not have a job and are irresponsible with money.

Below is an illustration of using a refund check wisely and a sample budget. Creating a budget will be super helpful for you in college and encourage you to get into the habit of budgeting after college.

TESHA'S EXAMPLE

We're about to do a little math in the following example to get your brain flowing and demonstrate a practical budget. For the most part, college students are typically broke. But you can always refer to some of those side hustles I mentioned earlier to help bring in extra cash, especially if you don't have financial support from your parents. Pay attention to the numbers and budget, how refund checks work, and the strategy to responsibly use the money. **This is only an example** for demonstration purposes! Your situation may vary drastically.

Tesha is a sophomore who is an out-of-state student and receives an academic scholarship that covers 100 percent of her tuition, books, and fees. She is awarded $4,000 in work-study, averaging about $2,000 per semester, and she's also a resident assistant. This means her housing and meal plan are covered.

While Tesha has a pretty little financial aid package, she's still thinking smart and strategically. She understands that she may still need funds for transportation, food, toiletries/personal items, electronics, and occasional entertainment. She creates a cost-of-living budget estimating what she will need each semester for her sophomore year. Each semester is about four months.

Tesha qualifies for the direct subsidized loan for $4,500 per academic year or $2,250 per semester. Since she has a scholarship and work-study to cover all of her student fees, she doesn't need the full amount of the loan, but she accepts it to invest and to assist with the rest of her living expenses since she does not have any financial support from home.

She can pocket a sizable refund check because her scholarship and work-study technically cover all school-related fees. Tesha understands that every loan needs to be paid back and that a loan is NOT free money. She understands the risk of incurring debt during her sophomore year but has a strategic and thoughtful plan.

Her loan is assessed an origination fee of 1 percent, which means she will technically net $2,227.50 per semester for the loan. This means Tesha will be able to pocket $847 in the fall after budgeted items and $2,147 for the spring after budgeted items. Therefore, she gets to keep $2,994 for the year from student loans and work-study refunds. See budget by semester below:

TESHA'S FALL SEMESTER BUDGET
EACH SEMESTER IS ABOUT FOUR MONTHS.

INCOME (FALL AWARDS)	
Federal loans (subsidized)	$2,227
Work-study	$2,000
Total Refund Check Amount	$4,227

FALL BUDGETED ITEMS BY MONTHLY COST

Groceries: Snacks for dorm $80

Dinner: Eating out off-campus 2x a week $140

Transportation: Off-campus outings (Ubers) $75

Travel for holidays: Flights not needed monthly

Toiletries: Stocks up at Dollar Store monthly $50

Nails/hair: Does her own hair. Mani/Pedi $75

Laptop/software: Work-study covers

Books/supplies: Scholarship covers

Entertainment: Games/concerts/parties $100

Emergency fund $125

TESHA'S FALL SEMESTER BUDGET
EACH SEMESTER IS ABOUT FOUR MONTHS.

INCOME (FALL AWARDS)	
Federal loans (subsidized)	$2,227
Work-study	$2,000
Total Refund Check Amount	$4,227

BUDGETED ITEMS	DETAILS	COST PER WEEK	COST PER MONTH	TOTAL
Groceries	Snacks for dorm	$20	$80	-$320
Dinner	Eating out off-campus 2x a week	$35	$140	-$560
Transportation	Off-campus outings (bus pass/ Uber)	-	$75	-$300
Travel home for holidays	Thanksgiving/Christmas flights	-	-	-$800
Toiletries/personal items	Stocks up at Dollar Store monthly	-	$50	-$200
Nails/hair	Does her own hair. Mani/Pedi 1x a month	-	$75	-$300
Laptop/ equipment/software	Work-study check will buy books/supplies	-	-	-$2000
Books /supplies	Covered by scholarship	-	-	-
Entertainment	Sports games, concerts, parties, outings, etc.	25	$100	-$400
Emergency fund	Screen crack, being stranded, or anything	-	$125	-$500

TOTAL FALL AMOUNTS
FALL SEMESTER BUDGET TOTAL -$3,380
FALL SEMESTER LEFTOVER FUNDS $847

SPRING BUDGETED ITEMS BY MONTHLY COST

Groceries: Snacks for dorm $80

Dinner: Eating out off-campus 2x a week $140

Transportation: Off-campus outings (Ubers) $75

Travel for holidays: Flights not needed monthly

Toiletries: Stocks up at Dollar Store monthly $50

Nails/hair: Does her own hair. Mani/Pedi $75

Laptop/software: Work-study covers

Books/supplies: Scholarship covers

Entertainment: Games/concerts/parties $100

Emergency fund $0

TESHA'S SPRING SEMESTER BUDGET

INCOME (SPRING AWARDS)	
Federal loans (subsidized)	$2,227
Work-study	$2,000
Total Refund Check Amount	$4,227

BUDGETED ITEMS	DETAILS	COST PER WEEK	COST PER MONTH	TOTAL
Groceries	Snacks for dorm	$20	$80	-$320
Dinner	Eating out off-campus 2x a week	$40	$160	-$560
Transportation	Off-campus outings: bus pass and Uber	-	$75	-$300
Toiletries/personal items	Stocks up at Dollar Store monthly	-	$50	-$200
Nails/hair	Does her own hair. Mani/Pedi once a month	-	$75	-$300
Books/supplies	Covered by scholarship	-	-	--
Entertainment	Sports games, concerts, parties, outings, etc.	$25	$100	-$400
Emergency Fund	Still had money from the fall semester	-	-	-

TOTAL SPRING AMOUNTS	
SPRING SEMESTER BUDGET TOTAL	-$2,080
SPRING SEMESTER LEFTOVER FUNDS	$2,147

PAYING FOR COLLEGE, SIDE HUSTLES, AND FINANCIAL FREEDOM TIPS

TESHA'S FALL SEMESTER BUDGET
EACH SEMESTER IS ABOUT FOUR MONTHS.

INCOME (FALL AWARDS)	
Federal loans (subsidized)	$2,227
Work-study	$2,000
Total Refund Check Amount	$4,227

BUDGETED ITEMS	DETAILS	COST PER WEEK	COST PER MONTH	TOTAL
Groceries	Snacks for dorm	$20	$80	-$320
Dinner	Eating out off-campus 2x a week	$35	$140	-$560
Transportation	Off-campus outings (bus pass/ Uber	-	$75	-$300
Travel home for holidays	Thanksgiving/Christmas flights	-	-	-$800
Toiletries/personal items	Stocks up at Dollar Store monthly	-	$50	-$200
Nails/hair	Does her own hair. Mani/Pedi 1x a month	-	$75	-$300
Laptop/ equipment/software	Work-study check will buy books/supplies	-	-	-$2000
Books /supplies	Covered by scholarship	-	-	-
Entertainment	Sports games, concerts, parties, outings, etc.	25	$100	-$400
Emergency fund	Screen crack, being stranded, or anything	-	$125	-$500
TOTAL FALL AMOUNTS			FALL SEMESTER BUDGET TOTAL	-$3,380
			FALL SEMESTER LEFTOVER FUNDS	$847

TESHA'S SPRING SEMESTER BUDGET

INCOME (SPRING AWARDS)	
Federal loans (subsidized)	$2,227
Work-study	$2,000
Total Refund Check Amount	$4,227

BUDGETED ITEMS	DETAILS	COST PER WEEK	COST PER MONTH	TOTAL
Groceries	Snacks for dorm	$20	$80	-$320
Dinner	Eating out off-campus 2x a week	$40	$160	-$560
Transportation	Off-campus outings: bus pass and Uber	-	$75	-$300
Toiletries/personal items	Stocks up at Dollar Store monthly	-	$50	-$200
Nails/hair	Does her own hair. Mani/Pedi once a month	-	$75	-$300
Books /supplies	Covered by scholarship	-	-	--
Entertainment	Sports games, concerts, parties, outings, etc.	$25	$100	-$400
Emergency Fund	Still had money from the fall semester	-	-	-
TOTAL SPRING AMOUNTS			SPRING SEMESTER BUDGET TOTAL	-$2,080
			SPRING SEMESTER LEFTOVER FUNDS	$2,147

Tesha has never had this much money all to herself before. While her friends are shopping and irresponsibly blowing their refund money, Tesha decides to be responsible. She has also read this book and learned about the dangers of getting into debt. Therefore, she decided to invest and save a portion of the $2,994 she received to help jump-start her future.

Tesha plans to get a job over the summer to save for a car and wants to use her vehicle to help establish credit and to prepare for a move off campus by senior year. Although Tesha has a full-ride scholarship, she is still actively applying for other scholarships (always), so she doesn't need to take out any additional loans. She's disciplined and refuses all credit card offers because she doesn't need them. Tesha is focused and set to have a very bright future.

After learning about the importance of investing, Tesha opens up a stockbroker account and funds her account with $2,500 of her refund check. She places the other $494 in a high-yield savings account if she needs to access it sooner. Tesha is learning to be pretty good with money and reads blogs, watches videos, and everything she can about building wealth. Regarding her refund check investments, she knows she has a limited window for her investment to yield maximum results on her subsidized loan.

The Department of Education pays the interest on subsidized loans while she is in school. She also has a six-month grace period after graduation before she has to begin paying this loan back. This would essentially give Tesha two years and six months to invest these funds interest-free.

If Tesha invests well, she will still have her original investment available and more by the time she's required to pay back the loan. By then, she plans to be employed and able to make payments. At that point, she can decide if she wants to keep the funds in her investment account and simply make direct monthly payments to her lender, or she can cash out her original investment to pay off her loan in full. Either way, it's a win-win, and she will get to keep any profits.

This sample story empowers you to apply for scholarships—enough where your tuition is covered, to be responsible, to think about creating your own budget, and to imagine how you can graduate from college debt-free. I highly recommend and encourage you to start researching and googling how to build wealth and the value of investing. There are so many tools out there, and you don't have to feel intimidated or like you need a lot of money to start.

You can start with $50 to $100. You'll easily blow this low amount on dinner, your nails, or your hair. Do the future you a favor and expand your knowledge! I WISH I knew a fraction of this as a college sophomore. I would have done things differently. But I'm passing this knowledge on to you, with love.

SAMPLE COLLEGE LIVING EXPENSES

I shared Tesha's story to provide insight into what you may need to pay for in college. In the example, Tesha is a sophomore living on campus and rent-free. She also had a meal plan under her position as an R.A. However, every student's living situation is different and will change each year as you prepare for graduation. Your budget will need to be tweaked according to what better fits your life and circumstances. Some students have savings, some parents send them money, some work jobs, and some have nothing

Some college students are very tight with their money, even cheap, and others (depending on their lifestyle before starting college) may want to maintain it. So, if Mama and Daddy kept you in the latest sneakers, hair/nails done and brand clothing, you will likely want to keep that going in college.

One thing for sure is that spending your own money is very different from spending your parents' money. The hard-earned dollar becomes more difficult to let go of so quickly, and it puts checks and balances in place, helping you determine if you really need something. Think about it: a $15 tab at Chick-fil-A could feel like the cost of a five-star dining experience when you only have $25 in your account.

Here's a word to the wise as you begin to navigate these highly overrated and ghetto adult streets. Spend wisely, look for ways to save, and ask yourself, do I need this, or do I want this? Not if you deserve it, but do you actually need it before swiping? In the real world, there is no one to come bail you out or pay your rent if you choose to party or fly to Mexico over spring break with your friends. If you work hard now and set yourself up for success when you graduate, you can create a lifestyle of playing harder and living the life you desire. Stay focused.

Added is a sample of Tesha's budget after she moved off campus. Her tuition and school fees are still covered under her academic scholarship. However, because she constantly applies for multiple other scholarships, she's awarded additional money.

Please note: Not every scholarship will allow you to keep additional funds if your tuition and fees are already covered. Meanwhile, some scholarships don't care what you do with the money because they send the award directly to the school. Other scholarships may only agree to cover a portion of living expenses associated with college while others will reduce the amount if you have enough aid to cover tuition.

Yes, you will still need money to live after paying college fees and tuition. So, whatever scholarships you are awarded, clarify with the provider if there are any stipulations.

The following chart is for illustration and educational purposes.

TESHA'S SENIOR YEAR BUDGET

Living expenses split with roommate are listed "RM"
Tesha's job income is calculated for 12 months.

INCOME SOURCE	PER MONTH	PER SEMESTER	PER YEAR
Scholarship Refund	$500	$2,000	$4,000
Work-study Refund	$1,250	$5,000	$10,000
Job Income	$1,400	$7,000	$16,800
Total Income Amount	$3,150	$14,000	$30,800

MONTHLY EXPENSES	BUDGETED	ACTUAL	COMMENTS
Rent	$700	$700	RM
Car note / Insurance	$450	$450	
Gas for car	$100	$75	Public transportation this month
Utilities	$100	$120	RM Electricity was higher this month
Internet	$15	$15	RM
Laundry	$25	$25	Stayed on budget
Groceries	$300	$300	Stayed on budget
Cell Phone	$75	$75	Doesn't change
Credit Cards	0	0	I don't use this
Medical Expenses	0	0	University and public health clinics
Parking/Uber	$30	$30	Split Uber with friends
Eating out/coffee	$100	$200	Over budget, ☹ friend's birthday
Entertainment	$200	$200	Stayed on budget
Home/personal	$50	$0	Didn't need anything this month
School expenses	$50	$0	Didn't need anything this month
Beauty/nails	$100	$100	Stayed on budget
Clothes	$150	$0	Under budget. Yay! Buy quarterly
Miscellaneous	$40	$40	Used for last-minute job lottery
TOTAL EXPENSES	**$2,485**	**$2,330**	

PER MONTH

TOTAL INCOME $3,150
TOTAL BUDGETED $2,485
TOTAL ACTUAL SPEND $2,330
LEFTOVER MONTHLY DIFFERENCE (INCOME – SPENDING) $820

TIPS FOR SAVING MONEY IN COLLEGE

Isn't Tesha sharp and financially responsible? Not only does she have a roommate by senior year (which is an excellent way to save), but she also stays within her monthly budget and doesn't use credit cards. She gets to add some of the $820 she had left to her investment and emergency savings account.

Tesha is doing a wonderful job with her money and setting herself up for an easier future. Guess what? Now that you've acquired all the stuff, I wish I knew, and what Tesha knows, you can even do better than her with your budgeting.

WAYS TO SAVE BEFORE COLLEGE
- Consider AP/dual enrollment in high school.
- Consider in-state and community colleges.
- Ask for cash at graduation and/or going-away parties.
- Save, Save, and SAVE!
- Get a part-time job and save.

WAYS TO SAVE WHILE IN COLLEGE
- Consider getting a part-time job.
- Get a roommate whenever possible.
- Eat on campus and look for ways to save.
- Avoid taking unnecessary classes and wasting money.
- Limit going out to 1-2x twice monthly (if it isn't free).
- Always ask for college discounts.
- Buy used textbooks or go in half with classmates.
- Avoid bringing a car to school unless you absolutely must.

CHAPTER SIX
THE SUMMER BEFORE

By this time, you should have already committed to a college and know where you're going. If you followed all the steps listed in the checklist and previous chapters, you should also know the amount of financial aid you're set to receive and are constantly applying for scholarships. If, for some reason, you're planning to enroll as a nontraditional student, meaning it's been some time since you graduated high school…no worries, I got you! There is a checklist for you as well.

This summer before starting college is all about balance, getting things in order, mentally preparing, but also having LOTS of fun! You may still be basking in the sweetness of a recent graduation, glowing with love, and filled with hope and excitement for your new adventure ahead. Then, on the flip side, maybe you're a bit anxious, nervous, and even a little scared. These are all totally normal emotions during this time of major transition.

The trick to enduring this process is to remain calm and lean in on your faith. You have to remember you ARE prepared and have everything you need, or you wouldn't be here. Little sis, you ARE divinely guided and ready for whatever life has in store for you.

Say it with me: I am divinely guided and prepared and have everything I need!

TRADITIONAL STUDENT SUMMER CHECKLIST:

1. Get Organized

Check your university's calendar, and if you haven't, start using the calendar on your phone. Mark all important dates listed on your college's website, like class registrations, orientation, housing deadlines, tuition/fee due dates, club sign-up deadlines, etc. You do not want to miss a deadline because you were disorganized and didn't know it. Your parents will not be around to hold your hand, and this is the perfect opportunity to start being more responsible.

If you don't know your Social Security number by heart, now is the time to memorize this and your student ID number. You will need it for all important college transactions and future transactions. I recommend getting a copy of this and your birth certificate as well.

You can create a folder (virtual or tangible) and add all your personal documents in this folder, including your Social Security card and your transcripts (be sure it's the final one). You want to write down or have your parents' socials as well, in case you have to deal with FAFSA. You may not need this, but it may be helpful to just have them on standby if you need them to verify anything. Make a copy of your driver's license or ID and add this as well.

I recommend putting these items in a locked and very secure place, or honestly, digitally in your secure cloud or Google folder is probably easier. Just make sure you secure your personal info. I can't say this enough with all the scams and hackers out there. Remember not to give your social number out randomly or click spam and suspect links in emails or on your phone. We will discuss safety later, but I just had to add that.

2. Revisit Financial Aid/Scholarships

Visit your financial aid package and check in with your school to ensure they don't need anything additional from you or your parents. Check to make sure all your financial aid awards are right. Also, check your scholarship spreadsheet frequently and keep looking and applying for free money that can be applied towards your tuition. Use the scholarship letter previously provided as often as needed and don't forget to update your status to incoming college freshmen.

Lastly, document everything you've applied for, check the status, and send follow-ups. Make sure your college has your final transcript after college graduation. If, for some reason, your school makes a mistake and doesn't send your transcript, a college can revoke your admission, even if it's not your fault, so it is very important to double-check that your last transcripts are on file at your school. Stay on top of this!

3. Consider Working Part-Time

Getting a part-time job is not only a great way to save money but also good for building relationships and possibly securing a job that you can return to over the holiday break and the following summer if you find it worthwhile.

4. Attend Summer Orientation/Get Plugged In, and Be Open

Summer orientation is one of the best ways to stay ahead of the curve while getting more one-on-one support before all the other freshmen come on campus. It is a great way to get acclimated to your school, to learn your way around, and to meet new people. Summer orientation is also a lot of fun because you don't technically have to start school the next day or right away, so you can mingle with others and learn about your university.

Lifelong friendships are often developed at orientation. Getting plugged in is pretty simple because you can meet some of your classmates virtually. Be sure to join Facebook class groups and look for hashtags related to your graduation class, city, and other affiliations you're a part of to meet other freshmen. Remember, they are all coming in new, just like you, and are also looking to meet people.

Don't put too much pressure into getting everything right. One of the best things you can do to avoid letting yourself down is to remove any expectations about anything, including how you think or want things to go with making friends or being in college. Avoid judging people you'll meet at orientation or anyone online. Trust me, you will see some things and people you may think are weird, but you are your own kind of weird, too.

If you come in thinking you know people or judging them, you may miss an opportunity to truly get to know people and build authentic and meaningful relationships. You're going to attract the same type of energy that you give off. So be kind, friendly, and open to different.

5. Square Away Housing and Connect with Your Roommate

After you have committed to a college, you'll need to figure out where you will be staying and what housing options are available for freshmen. This should be done as early as possible to avoid the nightmares associated with scrambling in the summer, just a month or so away from moving in. Make sure you pay your deposits and everything necessary to stay on top of housing, and have your parents make a personal connection with housing directors.

This is so important, especially if you are moving out of state or to an HBCU. Most college freshmen live in dorms or on-campus housing. This means you will have a roommate!

Roommates can be lots of fun, lifelong sister friends, but some experiences can be a nightmare. We will talk more about roommates later, but for now, see if your college allows you to pick roommates. If they do and you've connected with someone at orientation or virtually, you both can request each other.

You will want to choose carefully and ensure you are on the same page with cleaning, sleep times, and values. If you know who has been assigned to room with you, summer is a good time to speak about decorating, color schemes, or themes you may want for your room. You also want to decide and coordinate who will bring what.

6. Make a List of Your Needs and Shop

Summer is a great time to put the final touches on your list of needs, to make purchases, and to pack. You can ask family members to pitch in and help you get items on the list. If your family attends church, you can ask your church family for items on your list as well. Here are a few things you may need for sure: a laptop, microwave, fridge, cleaning supplies, clothing racks/hangers, and mattress covers. Again, don't forget to ask your roommate what she's bringing.

You can also consider having a trunk party. This is like a housewarming but for going away to college. Walmart, Target, and grocery store gift cards are also excellent items. Speaking of grocery stores, think about easy microwavable meals and snacks for your grocery list.

You will have a meal plan living in dorms and on campus, but there will be times when you may not want to eat at the campus café or when it closes too early. Being hungry and spending lots of money on Uber Eats is the worst. Therefore, if you already have some easy prep meals mapped out, you'll be prepared in advance.

Lastly, don't worry about buying all your books just yet. You want to first check in with your professors and read the syllabus to make sure you actually need them. Be sure to revisit your senior checklist in case you missed anything. Make sure you open a bank/savings account as well.

7. Have FUN

I can promise that so much will change from when you leave for college to when and if you return. You will see old high school classmates get married, have babies, and do big things; some will do the same things they did in high school. You will see people get buried and all types of evolution. With your family, you'll start to see all your aunts, uncles, and parents differently. Your perspective, feelings, and style will change, and life will go on in ways you probably never imagined.

One thing that is always sure in life is change, and because life is constantly evolving, it's so important for us to enjoy it, the moment, and the now! I once heard someone say it's not that life is too short; it's just that we wait too long to live it. Therefore, before you leave for college, commit to having fun and enjoying your family and friends.

Cherish all the moments you can with whomever you can because it's not promised that you will see them again. It may also be a couple of months before you can get back home unless you didn't go very far for college. Students who travel further usually don't return home until Thanksgiving or Christmas break, and that's about three months after you leave, so enjoy all the time you can with your loved ones—even your annoying little brother or sister and your annoying parents. You will miss them dearly.

8. Set Move-in Date

Make sure you're staying in contact with the housing team at your dorm or living quarters to set your move-in date and get there early. If you get there first, you will have first pick of the side of the room and bed you want. I recommend getting the bed furthest away from the door so others can't see your personal space whenever the door is open unless you're okay with this. You can also consider getting the bed closest to the bathroom for those late-night restroom runs. This comes in handy. Most schools encourage moving in a few days before orientation to get situated. Add your move-in date to your calendar!

UNTRADITIONAL STUDENT SUMMER CHECKLIST

☑ Create a folder (virtual or tangible) adding personal documents (Social Security numbers, transcripts, parents' Social/tax info (if necessary), and a copy of your DL or ID). Make sure this is safe and secure.

☑ Request copies of your high school transcript.

☑ Request copies of your previous test scores (ACT/SAT) if you took them. If not, there may be other proficient exams required.

☑ Contact the college you're considering, ask if exams or test scores are needed, and ask about specific requirements for non-traditional students.

☑ Apply for FAFSA (remember the deadline and that later applications may reduce aid amount. Be sure to identify as an independent student if you're eligible: 24 years or older, not claimed on parents' taxes, and other stipulations mentioned in previous chapters.

☑ Nonrefundable application fee.

☑ Complete the application and add any additional items the school requires as well.

☑ Apply for scholarships!

THE SUMMER BEFORE

FRESHMAN COLLEGE PURCHASE LIST

- Microwave (check with roommate first)
- Fridge (check with roommate first)
- Ironing board, curling irons, hair dryer
- Laptop/chargers and other electronics/heating pad
- Cleaning supplies/laundry supplies/toiletries
- Clothing/shoe racks
- Hangers
- Mattress covers/pad
- Bedsheets, covers/pillows/blankets, hair bonnet, etc.
- Underbed storage
- Full-length mirror
- Table lamp
- Clothes hamper
- Shower shoes
- Rug
- Backpack/folders, paper, and any school supplies
- Room decorations
- Clothing
- Bathroom caddy
- Towels/robes

CHAPTER SEVEN

ORIENTATION, CLASS SELECTION, GRAD PLANS, AND THE FIRST SEMESTER

Before attending orientation, whether in summer or fall, it's important to remain open-minded, knowing that this experience will be different. Remember to give yourself some grace and keep your primary goal (to graduate) and the plan of action to get you there in mind. Your graduation plan is the path you'll take and the plan you'll follow to get you to the finish line of either an associate's, certificate, or bachelor's degree. Having a plan helps to prevent taking unnecessary classes and spending unnecessary money.

Because your college experience will be life-changing, with lots of learning, unlearning, and loads of fun, it's important to make sure you balance and handle your business first. That is the business of keeping your grades up, avoiding trouble, learning as much as possible, and preparing for graduation. Hopefully, by now, you have decided if you will attend full-time or part-time.

If you're looking to graduate in four years, being a full-time student is the fastest way to get you to graduation. Full-time students are students taking 12 or more credit hours per semester. However, taking up to 15 or 16 hours each semester is ideal to finish in four years.

You can take up to 18 hours a semester, but that would be considered a really heavy load and not advised for a freshman. Anything more than 16 hours is not recommended or smart, either. Taking too many hours as a newbie can be stressful, and we want to avoid unnecessary stress. I understand that this may sound foreign and counting credit hours is confusing, but we'll go over a sample schedule so that you'll have a better understanding.

15 THINGS TO CONSIDER GOING INTO YOUR FIRST SEMESTER

- Don't wait until the last minute to register or you will have a schedule that you probably will hate, including early morning and evening classes.

- Finalize your class schedule and decide sooner rather than later if you will keep your schedule or drop classes.

- If you're not a morning person, do not register for 8 a.m. classes.

- Meet with your academic advisor and introduce yourself to your professors during their office hours.

- Meet with your financial aid advisor and make sure there are no holds on your account and that your financial aid is enough to cover the year.

- Even if you were an overachiever in high school, be mindful that college is a new experience, and you don't want to overwhelm yourself with too many challenging classes in the same semester. For example, taking chemistry, physics, and advanced algebra all at once may be a headache and very demanding. So be sure to spread out the hard classes among the easy ones.

- Don't buy your textbooks right away. Read the syllabus and check in with the professor to see if they plan to actually use the textbooks or if an older edition of that book is sufficient. Older editions are cheaper.

- Make sure you balance your gen-eds with other classes.

- Enroll in electives that you actually like and learn about what's happening on campus and what resources are offered to you.

- Start light and ease into it, so beginning with 12 hours is good for your first semester unless you have an odd-number credit hour class; 13 or 14 is fine too.

- Find your ideal quiet space to study and create a routine and calendar to help with time management (check out my website for complimentary resources).

- Figure out the campus layout and which buildings your classes are in, in advance.

- Don't be late to class, and be sure to factor in transportation, and the weather, if you need to walk far or take a shuttle bus.

- Don't be so thirsty and eager to drive or bring a car the first semester. Cars are not recommended for freshman year, and they can be a hassle with decals, paying for parking, or repairs.

- Connect with other students on campus.

Let's talk about registration and your graduation plan. Registration is typically done in or right after orientation with the support of your academic advisor. Your advisor may register you for the first semester, but it is up to you after this. When registering, you will review the semester's classes and select classes according to your graduation plan. Sometimes, your advisor will be stretched thin with hundreds of other students. Therefore, knowing how to plot your graduation plan for yourself is so important if it's difficult to get on your advisor's calendar immediately.

DROPPING AND ADDING CLASSES

Typically, within the first few weeks of school, you'll be able to gauge whether your schedule and classes will be a good fit for you. There will be times when you may need to drop a class. For example, you get into a class and later realize you don't like your professor's teaching style or that it's difficult to follow. Additionally, you have multiple classes that require more than you have the capacity to give, or you forgot to register for a specific class that's necessary and only offered seldomly, and you need to drop. Whatever your reasons for schedule changes are, there will be a short window of time for your school to allow these changes.

Please check with your advisor about when this timeframe ends and if there are penalties associated with this. For example, you can receive a full refund for the dropped class if done before a specific day. Unlike high school, any dropped courses do not appear on your transcripts. However, your financial aid can be negatively impacted if you drop too many classes or if your dropped classes change your status from full-time to part-time because your hours dropped down to 11. So be sure you have a solid reason for dropping and that your academic advisor is helping you select a proper class to replace what you dropped.

See the sample graduation plan. Each major and degree requirement will differ based on your school and program. Mapping out a plan in advance helps determine if you will graduate in four years or less or more.

Remember we previously talked about per credit hours and how each graduation plan requires a unique amount of hours/credits to get your degree? Your tuition includes the cost of each class, including the per credit hour cost.

Disclaimer: The sample graduation plan is only for demonstration purposes and is not intended to mirror your school. I am providing this to give you insight into how your degree plan will work and to encourage you to think about ways to complete school in a balanced and strategic way. Please work with your academic advisor for specific registration requirements for your program.

SAMPLE GRADUATION PLAN
4-Year Communications Degree Plan
120 Hours Needed to Graduate with Bachelor's Degree (Full Time)

Add any AP, IB, or early college credits (these are credits you earned in high school)_____

MAJOR COURSE
- ☑ 30 credit hours

CONCENTRATION COURSE
- ☑ 24 credit hours

GEN-ED COURSES = 45 CREDIT HOURS NEEDED

- ☑ 9 hours of English
- ☑ 3 hours of math
- ☑ 6 hours of science
- ☑ 3 hours of language/philosophy/culture
- ☑ 3 hours of creative arts
- ☑ 6 hours of American history
- ☑ 6 hours of government/political science
- ☑ 3 hours of social/behavioral science
- ☑ 6 hours of institutional options

ELECTIVES COURSE
- ☑ 21 credit hours

With the help and advisement of your academic advisor, you will be provided a curriculum summary and a list of classes to choose from to satisfy the necessary hours in each of the sections listed. There may be instances where your advisor is not on top of this with you, so it's always helpful to know your degree plan and what's needed independently. Be sure you register early and have a good balance of challenge and enjoyment.

Major hours are the number of hours needed in your major. These are specific study areas. Your school will offer a list of required classes based on your major.

Concentration hours are an area of emphasis within your major. Your school will offer a list of approved classes to choose from. For example, your major may be communications, but your concentration might be radio, TV and film, or your major may be biology, but your concentration is veterinary studies because you want to be a vet. I hope this makes sense.

General education hours are what we talked about—all the gen-ed classes at the college level. For example, these are the first parts of your degree before entering your major and concentration area. These can be math, English, and science classes.

Elective hours are classes where you get to choose to learn in different areas that interest you and to enjoy some flexibility, just like in high school.

To finish 120 hours in 8 semesters (not including summer), your schedule may look like this:

FRESHMAN YEAR SAMPLE GRADUATION PLAN
4-Year Communications Degree Plan
120 Hours Needed to Graduate with Bachelor's Degree
(Full Time)

	FALL SEMESTER		**SPRING SEMESTER**	
	COURSE INFORMATION	CREDIT HOURS	COURSE INFORMATION	CREDIT HOURS
FRESHMAN YEAR	ENGL 1301 Freshman English I	3	ENGL 1302 Freshman English II	3
	MATH 1314 College Algebra	3	COMM 1315 Public Address OR COMM 1321 Business & Professional Comm	3
	BIOL 1308 Survey of Life Science	3	GEOL 1303 Introduction to the Earth	3
	HIST 1301 Soc and Pol Hist U.S. to 1877	3	POLS 2305 American Government	3
	Choose from: ARTS 1315 Intro African Art OR THEA 1310 Introduction to Theatre OR MUSI 131 Introduction to Music	3	Choose from: PSYC 2301 General Psychology OR SOCI 1301 Introduction to Sociology OR SOCI 1306 Contemporary Social Issues	3
	TOTAL HOURS : 15		**TOTAL HOURS : 15**	

ORIENTATION, CLASS SELECTION, GRAD PLANS, AND THE FIRST SEMESTER

SOPHOMORE YEAR SAMPLE GRADUATION PLAN
4-Year Communications Degree Plan
120 Hours Needed to Graduate with Bachelor's Degree
(Full Time)

SOPHOMORE YEAR

FALL SEMESTER		SPRING SEMESTER	
COURSE INFORMATION	CREDIT HOURS	COURSE INFORMATION	CREDIT HOURS
Choose from:		COSC 1301 Intro to Computer Science I	3
ENGL 2326 American Literature	3		
or		COMM 200 Intro to Media Research Tech	3
ENGL 2328 African-American Literature	3	COMM 220 Media Literacy	3
or			
ENGL 2332 World Literature I	3	COMM 221 Intercultural Communication	3
or			
ENGL 2333 World Literature II	3	Elective	3
POLS 2306 Texas Government	3		
COMM 130 Introduction to Comm Studies			
HIST 1302 Soc and Pol Hist U.S. Since 1877			
COMM 232 Interpersonal Communication			
TOTAL HOURS : 15		TOTAL HOURS : 15	

COLLEGE BOUND: A BLACK GIRL'S GUIDE

JUNIOR/SENIOR YEAR SAMPLE GRADUATION PLAN
4-Year Communications Degree Plan
120 Hours Needed to Graduate with Bachelor's Degree
(Full Time)

	FALL SEMESTER		**SPRING SEMESTER**	
	COURSE INFORMATION	CREDIT HOURS	COURSE INFORMATION	CREDIT HOURS
JUNIOR YEAR	COMM 332 Computer Applications in Communication	3	COMM 330 Professional Development & Ethics	3
	COMM 336 Comm Research Design	3	COMM 331 Persuasion	3
	COMM 337 Media Criticism	3	Concentration Course	3
	Concentration Course	3	Concentration Course	3
	Elective	3	Elective	3
	TOTAL HOURS : 15		TOTAL HOURS : 15	
SENIOR YEAR	COMM 439 Experiential Learning	3	Concentration Course	3
	Concentration Course	3	Concentration Course	3
	Elective	3	Concentration Course	3
	Concentration Course	3	Elective	3
	Elective	3	Elective	3
	TOTAL HOURS : 15		TOTAL HOURS : 15	

A TOTAL OF FOUR YEARS (8 SEMESTERS) = HOURS 120

I hope this sample is helpful. I promise it will make more sense when you register for freshman year. Again, you'll choose from a list of classes according to your degree plan, and with the help of your freshman-year advisor, you'll build a balanced and strategic schedule. You'll continue doing this until you graduate. Remember to always register early, so inquire each semester about when registration opens so you're not stuck with a crappy class schedule!

The easiest way to ensure you graduate in four years is to take 15 hours minimum each semester. You can also consider taking classes in the summer if you want to graduate early. Just be mindful that financial aid is not always available in the summer. Therefore, double-check and speak with your financial aid advisor to request summer aid and to make sure there is aid available.

SURVIVING THE FIRST FEW WEEKS AND SEMESTER

The electric atmosphere at HBCUs during those first few weeks is insane. I'm sure this is also the case at PWIs, but I can only speak from a personal HBCU experience in this section. Granted, the first few weeks and semester for a freshman on any campus should be filled with excitement! Those first few months are your time to shine. I'll start with what I know about HBCUs, and since you're a part of the culture, you know how some of your cousins get down.

First semester, you'll see lots of fashion, foolishness, and Black excellence, and you'll learn who's who and how to network and keep up fast. There will be lots of random parties, kickbacks, socials, barbeques, pep rallies, and turn-ups in the middle of the day. Yes, parties in the middle of the day and afternoon. If you're new to the city, you'll learn quickly where the nearest Walmart resides (Tarjay probably won't be in the budget) and who on campus has access to wheels. There will always be someone with wheels in your dorm.

You will learn that the "yard" or "quad" is the epicenter of the campus but also a fashion show, the place to kick it and post up. At HBCUs, the band is everything, and band members take their jobs seriously. You may hear them well into midnight rehearsing on campus before a game.

Homecoming is the biggest event of the semester because it's literally what it means, but it's way better than high school. I'm a little biased, but homecoming in college is really for alumni as it welcomes all former students to come back on campus. It's basically a family reunion at HBCUs, but it will also be lots of fun for you.

You may see random celebrities on campus at any time, and the café is usually bussin', meaning the food is fire. Most of your professors will feel like distant aunties and uncles. And the rivalry between other HBCUs seems real, but honestly, they're just for fun, kind of like cousin or sibling rivalry.

If you decide to attend an HBCU, don't come in with assumptions and think you know what it's like. Although predominantly Black, there is a wealth of diversity among students from different cities, religions, cultures, backgrounds, and economic statuses. The best advice is to be open, curious and engaged.

If attending a PWI, there will also be a variety of parties and events on campus for those first few weeks. Many schools host something called Welcome Week, which is set up to intentionally help new students feel connected and welcomed on campus. There will also usually be a big game as well. During welcome week, many upperclassmen help freshmen acclimate to new campus life. Please attend as many events and opportunities as possible to learn more about your school and student body.

Speaking of upperclassmen, here is a sidenote that I need to share because I genuinely care about you, your heart, your reputation, and the future legacy you'll leave on and off campus. Setting boundaries with yourself and others will be very important in your first few weeks. You will train people how to treat you. People will treat you accordingly if you demand respect, treat people well, and honor your boundaries.

Remember I opened this book talking about identity? I did this on purpose because if you go to school unaware of yourself and your standards, there is a higher chance for you to be eaten alive. And I'm talking about becoming something you're not, chasing clout, doing things you normally wouldn't, and acting out of character. Girls who start off like this not only make a poor name for themselves but are also more likely to struggle in class because they don't have focus.

Please try not to get caught up in the hype of having freedom and doing things you wouldn't normally do, especially if this is your first time away from home. If you start off making bad decisions, chances are you will continue, or you will have a harder time turning things around. Remember the type of woman you said you wanted to be? Always keep her in mind and use her character as your barometer. For example, tell yourself this: the type of woman I want to be wouldn't do _____ or engage in _____ because she has high standards.

During my freshman year, I distinctly remember hearing friends and people telling me nobody cares what you do when you get to college; you're basically grown. If that wasn't the worst advice I got, I don't know what was.

Admittedly, I was boy-crazy and so ready to leave home and enjoy some freedom. On my first day on campus (before orientation), I was mesmerized by all the athletes, fraternity guys, and upperclassmen. I didn't know it, but many of them intentionally preyed on freshman girls. I fell instantly for this one football player who was an upperclassman and habitual liar who also talked to other girls, including girls in my dorm that I had no clue about. Although that was well over twenty years ago, guys still do the same thing today.

All this to say, be smart, mindful, and observant of people's actions (men and women) vs. what they say. People will tell you anything but watch their behaviors closely. You'll also meet shady girl "friends" with hidden motives. During those first weeks, you will be faced with tough decisions of not falling victim to peer pressure, feeling awkward about not knowing many people, balancing freedom, and living with a roommate you truly don't know unless you get lucky.

There will be a slew of parties, events, accessible drugs, and alcohol, and people recording everything and doing all types of weird things. My advice is if you have to question something that doesn't sit or feel right with your gut, don't do it, and don't go. You don't owe anyone anything! Remember why you're really there, which is to graduate. And as long as you prioritize homework, studying, and classes, having a little fun is important, too, but the kind of fun you won't be ashamed of.

STAYING BALANCED AND AHEAD THE FIRST SEMESTER

Overall, that first semester will fly by quickly. It's usually only fifteen weeks, just shy of four months. It's like all the hype getting you in, getting your schedule, getting started, navigating all the parties, events, personal and social things, **midterms**, more events, parties, personal and social things, and lastly, **finals**. And that's semester one in a nutshell; yep, it's a rinse and repeat. The true key is mastering balance, staying grounded, and discovering new things about yourself.

You will survive and thrive if you stay on top of your studies, be real and honest with yourself, stay in touch with your professors, keep those grades up, keep God in the center, and stay focused. College, in many ways, is really about adapting, learning, maturing, and cultivating who you want to be in the real world and what you need to be successful when you get there.

I will use this section to reiterate a little bit of what I mentioned in the early chapters with the survival checklist and expound on the purpose and necessity of this book. While there are other mainstream college prep books, they do not explicitly speak to YOU, addressing some of the unique challenges and issues facing young Black women. *College Bound: A Black Girl's Guide* is written specifically with you in mind.

The book isn't about divisiveness at all! It's about ensuring that you are considered, aware, and equipped with specific knowledge that will prepare you for college and life beyond. This time can be exciting, overwhelming, and intimidating for everyone involved, including your parents and loved ones. For Black girls specifically, this time is critical for cultivating your identity, identifying and owning your purpose, developing skills, and learning as much as possible to mitigate future risks of intersectionality (racism, sexism, inequalities, and other disadvantages) that could create unnecessary obstacles for your future. **My heart for this book is to provide a safe space for you, Black girl**, to feel seen and heard while preparing to position yourself as a leading authority for life after college.

HBCU/PWI SURVIVAL CHECKLIST
BGAP (Black Girls at PWIs)

☑ Develop a prayer life and bring God on campus with you.
☑ Be proactive when handling your business and hold people accountable.
☑ Learn as much as you can and take initiative.
☑ Read your syllabus, ask questions, and never wait for your instructors to tell you what to do.
☑ Remember, your goal is to graduate.
☑ Take advantage of all the facilities (library, rec, gym, etc.) because you are paying for them.
☑ Do not procrastinate, and demonstrate consistency, discipline, and self-control.
☑ Meet new people and always be open.
☑ Be choosy and mindful of the company you keep.
☑ Please avoid credit cards!
☑ Always apply and look for scholarship money.

BLACK GIRLS AT PWIS
☑ Always remember that you are worthy and deserve to be wherever you are.
☑ Your authenticity is most helpful, valuable, and necessary over anything else!
☑ Be confident in who you are, and don't fold, dim your light, or pretend to be something you are NOT.
☑ Don't allow people to mispronounce your name, say slick/inappropriate things (about you or in your presence).
☑ Don't let anyone touch your hair or invade your personal space.

ORIENTATION, CLASS SELECTION, GRAD PLANS, AND THE FIRST SEMESTER

- ☑ Learn about microaggressions, tone policing, gaslighting, covert racism, and other discriminatory behaviors.
- ☑ It's okay to be angry at times (all humans experience this) and to demonstrate emotion but do it appropriately.
- ☑ You don't have to prove yourself or try to be "strong," and it is not your responsibility to represent an entire race.
- ☑ Connect with people who celebrate you.
- ☑ Find your people and get tapped in with any Black student unions and organizations or create one if necessary.
- ☑ Keep an open mind and heart, extending grace to yourself and others.
- ☑ Always look for learning and teaching opportunities to educate yourself and others.
- ☑ Uncomfortable communication doesn't have to be super confrontational.
- ☑ Be direct with your professors and advisors, and don't accept handouts not offered to everyone else.
- ☑ Be sure to speak up, advocate for yourself, set boundaries, and report any incidents if and when they happen.
- ☑ You train people how to treat you.
- ☑ Don't assume every Black person on campus is your friend.

CAREER TIPS TO MAKE FRESHMAN YEAR A SUCCESS

- Your GPA is your current leverage, so keep your grades up and learn as much as possible in all areas, even outside your major.

- Focus more on what you want to DO instead of thinking about job titles and what you want to BE.

- Learn as much as you can about technology and digital skills (content creation, e-comm, network/info security, digital marketing, social media marketing, and data analytics). This is the new wave and helpful in future roles.

- Create a LinkedIn profile and résumé and start establishing yourself as a professional.

- Always look for opportunities to study abroad and seek opportunities to volunteer when you can. Use your summer/spring breaks wisely. If you get a job, apply for jobs where you will be challenged and learn valuable things.

- Research transferable skills and work to gain some of these.

- Identify the value that you know you can add, work to strengthen this, and own it.

- Position yourself for internships immediately by keeping a high GPA and applying.

- Be mindful of your digital fingerprints and all the messages you are putting out to the world on social media.

- Stay plugged into the career center on campus for opportunities, read books and blogs, and watch videos that align with your field to stay knowledgeable.

FRESHMAN ROUTINE
Recommended morning routine

- Make your bed
- 15 minutes of prayer / meditation
- 5-10 minute stretch
- Brush teeth and wash your face
- Shower and get dressed
- Affirmations (in the mirror helps)
- Please eat something!
- 10 minute social media / news
- Check emails
- Review today's schedule
- Write to-do list for today
- Arrive to class five mins early

ORGANIZER CHECKLIST
Recommended focus areas

- Review syllabus weekly
- Keep my GPA up
- Study and double-check due dates
- Intentionally learn new things
- Stay organized
- Build and nurture relationships
- Complete required reading
- Be intentional about self-care
- Rest and work out
- Career planning and forecasting
- Dental cleaning and annual woman's wellness
- Check on my family
- Apply for scholarships
- Save money and make money

I'm glad that you now know what a grad plan is and what to expect that first semester. The other seven semesters through graduation will be a rinse and repeat, meaning you'll do it repeatedly. But the cool part is that you'll be different (wiser and more confident) every time, each semester until graduation.

I want to close this chapter with this. While your first semester is important (setting the stage for your college career), how you finish is more important. I say this as encouragement in case you don't get off to a good start.

Little sis, you will experience some difficulties (personally and professionally) this first semester. This is normal for any new thing you face in life; there will be learning curves because you've never been here before. So be kind to yourself in the process, but also clear about who you want to become.

Do all the things that the woman you want to be would do, even when no one is watching (you are, and God sees you). Self-love is treating you well, honoring, and respecting yourself. You owe it to yourself to honor what you set out to do. Be sure to have some fun this semester as well!

Over the next few chapters, I'll provide insight to drive the overall point home. We want to ensure you are prepared for graduation and set up for success financially, mentally, physically, and academically.

CHAPTER EIGHT

KEEPING YOUR GRADES UP AND TIME MANAGEMENT

You are at a point in your life where no one is coming to save you or remind you to study and do your homework. Success academically and in life takes dedication, discipline, focus, and lots of effort. Discipline doesn't care if you are tired, how you feel, stayed up too late, or partied too hard. Discipline is doing all the things you don't want to do because they are what you need to do.

I've mentioned this before, and I will say it again. Your GPA as a student is all you have to show for. It is really important, and it does matter in college. Think about watching a basketball game in the fourth quarter, and the score is 112 to 70. Although the team with 70 points trained all week and worked really hard, no one can see that, nor will they consider this. All that matters is the points they're putting up. The score provides a glimpse of what's happening on the court and the team's offense/defense and application.

Just like your GPA, but you are playing a game against yourself. Your grade point average is a measuring tool that reflects how well you're doing, applying yourself, and your ability to remain resilient. It provides a glimpse into your ability to reflect the information you've retained.

Your GPA can impact your marketability when applying for scholarships, internships, and even seeking employment. Your GPA determines if you will graduate. If you're being lazy, nonchalant, and C'ing your way through school, barely applying yourself and not caring, what employer will want to hire you?

Most importantly, why waste thousands of dollars to be average? You were created for and deserve the best of the best, so you owe it to yourself to keep your grades up. To be clear, I am referring to you going hard, giving your all, and doing what you can. Moreover, there will be times when classes are extremely challenging and a C is all you can muster up, but you've applied yourself and given it your all.

In cases like this, don't be too hard on yourself. But don't use it as a cop-out, either. If you identify you need additional support, please make sure you get it. There are resources on campus that you are paying for (in your tuition), including your professor's salaries, so tap into help as you need it. Below are a couple of ways to boost your GPA, stand out, and perform at your highest to ensure success in class.

1. **Take What You Need**

It's not uncommon to feel trapped in super challenging classes and to later find out that you never needed them in the first place. Therefore, be sure to register for and take classes that you ONLY need. Your graduation plan can help you stay on top of this. Stay in close contact with your advisor for feedback. Your advisor will know of some classes that are eligible for substitutions. It makes no sense to waste energy and brain power on something you don't need, so only take what you need. You can consider taking easy and fun electives that will help to boost your GPA as well.

2. **Get an Understanding**

Growing up, you probably heard this phrase: "The only stupid question is the one you didn't ask." I couldn't agree more. Then there is this Bible passage in Proverbs 4:7 that says the beginning of wisdom is to acquire wisdom. In everything you do, make sure you get an understanding. That's my paraphrase that basically says you have to make sure you understand.

I think pride keeps people from understanding because who hates feeling slow or like they don't catch on easily? It's totally okay to not know something. We all are on different levels and learn differently. And instructors teach differently. I can't tell you how many classes I had with foreign professors who taught differently with English as a second language. It was tough and necessary for me to visit their office hours to have them personally break things down. Yes, it was a little embarrassing and took more of my time, but it was necessary.

When a professor also sees you actually trying, they may be more lenient when it's time to submit those grades. So, make sure you get a FULL understanding of what is expected and avoid winging assignments, papers, and quizzes. You can't be successful at something you don't understand or that you are winging, nor can you afford not to.

3. **Get Cool with Advisors/Professors**

Professors will have office hours where they are required to be available to support you in the success of their classes. Your professor and academic advisor should be on the same page, and it's your responsibility to build relationships with them to ensure you get what you need to be successful. They've been in your shoes and are equipped with strategies and resources to help you get through and excel in the class.

Always ask for feedback in class and ask questions, too. When they give you feedback, make sure you apply it. You want to stand out and leave a mark, so your professor knows you well. Building relationships is vital for everything. I will talk more about relationships and networking later, but I'm telling you, this works.

I had the privilege of being asked to film special assignments off campus and received recommendations for scholarships and opportunities because of the rapport I built with my advisor and professors. Every time I needed help, getting the support I needed was never a problem, especially facing difficult assignments. Because of my relationships, I could also request deadline extensions when needed. I'm not saying be a brownnoser or suck up. I am saying to be smart because your professor has something you need: your grade and ability to help you get your degree.

4. Use Resources and Get Tutoring

Check with the career center, academic advisor, or your department for tutoring support, or see who tutors in your dorm. Having a tutor is helpful in many ways to boost your GPA. Especially if they are a peer tutor, they will be able to speak to you in a language you understand and break things down more easily.

Take advantage of this and see what other tutoring or mentoring options the school offers. I always advise clarifying your needs and taking notes on why and what is challenging for you so you can articulate this to your tutor. What has you feeling insecure, and what concepts are not registering for you? If you can identify where your disconnect is, that can help you tackle the need more effectively. Consider watching YouTube videos or other resources on your struggle areas.

5. Be Proactive

Setting intentions and goals helps to save time, energy, and the likelihood of higher grades. I like to use the analogy of riding around without a destination. What happens when you hop in the car without a destination? You're going to waste gas if you don't know where you're going. Like most people who start up their car, they have an idea of where they want to go. This is the same with your classwork and GPA. After identifying where you want to go, you'll think through what you need to get there and then go for it.

A major stress reliever in "going for it" is working in advance, allowing yourself enough time, and turning things in on time. Think about it. Suppose you set a goal to have your work completed by a certain date, and you start your assignment early. In that case, you will not only finish early, but it also takes a load of stress and anxiety off. Also, consider arriving to class a bit early to ensure you're on time and to proactively get your work done. One way to get an easier A is to turn your work in on time and avoid points off for lateness. This gives you breathing room.

If you know you will be traveling or out, be proactive and speak with your professors in advance to tie loose ends. This is a part of handling your business. Give yourself more time in case you need more time. You can also visit www.rahkalshelton.com/collegebound for additional goal-setting resources.

6. Study Groups

Studying in groups is a big thing in college; at least, it was for me, and I led a couple of them. These can be fun, a great way to make friends and to bond together. Connecting with classmates allows you to gain another's perspective, insight, and approach to the work. Often, something will be said that sparks a breakthrough or new idea for you. Study groups can also provide emotional support and encouragement to one another, especially if the professor is challenging. Your groupmates will totally understand and get you. Don't be afraid to start one if there isn't one existing in your classes.

7. Stay Organized and Take Notes

You know you better than anyone else, and you should know by now the type of learner you are. If you're more hands-on, visual, or audible with learning, make sure you set yourself up for success that speaks to your unique learning style. Having systems and being organized will help tremendously.

I know you've seen the "O" word over and over in this book. Organization is just a life hack. Even if you're not the brightest, being organized can help you go further than some of your smartest classmates. I highly recommend you take notes, organize them, and know what to anticipate next.

One of the easiest ways that has worked for me with note-taking is paraphrasing. I paraphrase each page of reading back to myself with examples and stories that I follow. For reading that's very dense and hard to follow, I had to paraphrase by paragraph. It was a lot, but it helped me in areas I struggled with. I would notate lightly in pencil in the margin of my book (so I could erase it easily if I wanted to sell my books later) or on paper. You can also do this on your phone, tablet, or whatever electronic gadget you like.

I am a habitual notetaker even now. I take notes on my phone or in Google Documents and organize things by folders. You can consider making a folder for freshman year and then break this down into subfolders for the fall and spring semesters. In those folders, break down each class and then add notes per class. That will help you get organized. You can also do it old school with a binder and color-coded tabs per class.

Whatever your preference, just make sure you take solid notes during instructional time. Also, consider recording your class lectures so you can go back and listen to them later. Being organized can totally boost your confidence in class. Lastly, keep all your previous assignments that had 90% and up. And study what you did previously to earn those A's. Look back at your older notes and your previous methods of success as well. You did something right and can take a page from your own book.

8. Discipline and Effort

I mentioned that discipline doesn't care how you feel, and it doesn't. Being disciplined is making a decision not to be average or reactive. Truthfully, this separates most unsuccessful people from others: their discipline and work ethic. If you really want to boost your GPA and be extraordinary, you must do the work required for this. It's hard, no doubt, but available to those who want it.

Here's a popular Army phrase, "Proper planning and preparation prevents piss poor performance." This phrase is pretty self-explanatory. A famous poet and writer by the name of Johann Wolfgang Von Goethe said, "To think is easy. To act is hard. But the hardest thing in the world is to act in accordance with your thinking." [9] This is why everything mentioned previously is so important. Staying organized, being proactive, having study groups, using resources, taking what you need, and building relationships are all a part of your strategy and framework for encouraging a higher GPA.

---

[9] Johann Wolfgang von Goethe > Quotes > Quotable Quote, goodreads, https://www.goodreads.com/quotes/21696-to-think-is-easy-to-act-is-hard-but-the.

If you're thinking successfully, being disciplined, and putting in true effort, there is no way you won't see a difference. Putting in the hard work and effort will reflect in your grades. In college, you don't get graded for effort; but your effort is visible in your GPA. Furthermore, the higher this is, the better you'll be set up for opportunities and success in and beyond college.

STRATEGIES FOR DIFFICULT PROFESSORS

Because people are people with different values, backgrounds, and perspectives, we won't always vibe with everyone's style. In life, there's a possibility you'll be faced with working with a difficult supervisor, coworker, classmate, boss, and even professor. When this happens, you'll need to be mindful of that fine line between being firm and flexible, especially when the challenge is with a person who has authority or something you need.

Let's say you're stuck with a hard-nosed professor who grades really tough, has unrealistic expectations, and an insane syllabus, and you need this class. What do you do? You can do a couple of things to keep your peace and dignity without feeling like you have to kiss up to him or her.

1. Aim to get on the same page and meet with the professor to build a rapport and relationship and understand their expectations.
2. Express your concerns with your department chair and keep a paper trail of any issues you've had with the professor in case the level-set conversation gets you nowhere (you can email things to yourself just for a time stamp and logging purposes). You may not need this, but you'll have it for later if you need to dispute an unfavorable grade.

3. Connect with others in that class for support and strategies.
4. Focus on the class material as best as possible, not the professor.
5. You can limit your interactions and keep them cordial and professional, giving them what they're asking for. Fortunately, you won't have them too long.

TIME MANAGEMENT/PROCRASTINATION/URGENT VS. IMPORTANT

Think of a time when you had a paper, chore, or assignment due. You knew about it in advance but chose to wait until the last minute to get started. Besides being pressed and not your very best, how did that last-minute rush make you feel, and how did things work out? Don't tell me you work better under pressure...seriously! Placing yourself in unnecessary stress-induced situations isn't wise, even if you feel you do work better under pressure.

Waiting to the last minute often communicates a few things, including I don't respect what was asked of me, I don't take it seriously, or I don't respect my own time. I know this sounds harsh, but it's a difficult truth. However, we wait until the last minute for a few other reasons. This is called procrastination, and procrastination isn't our friend. It is the nemesis of effective time management. It even shows up disguised at times.

Most people procrastinate for these reasons:

1. They don't understand, know how to, or are intimidated by something.
2. They don't want to do it in the first place.

3. They don't respect what's asked of them, the other person's time, or their own time.
4. It will require more than they can give at the moment.
5. It's super easy; they can knock it out quickly.

For my "I just work better under pressure" people, the root of your lagging falls into one of the categories mentioned above. However, what's really happening when people say they work better under pressure is that the brain is registering deadlines as threats, releasing adrenaline and cortisol. The release of these chemicals can produce energy to activate, move, and to get going. But with this cortisol and adrenaline boost, if one thing goes wrong, that under-pressure high can easily turn into anxiety, leading to bigger problems. I recommend identifying if, when, and why you're procrastinating and then creating a strategy to attack it.

Before we break down and address procrastination roots, I want to briefly share the difference between urgent and important. Knowing the difference and acting accordingly can save significant time and help reinforce healthy time management. Time management is the process of organizing and planning how to divide your time between different activities. With strong time management, you can work a lot smarter vs. harder, getting so much more done in less time. This is why rooting out procrastination and identifying the difference between urgent and important is key.

Urgent tasks, activities, and needs are those that are time-sensitive and require your immediate attention to avoid negative immediate consequences. Important tasks, activities, and things are vital but do not require a stop-what-you-are-doing response. Often, we confuse urgent and important. Everything feels urgent, especially in social media, notifications, text messaging, and instant culture.

TIME MANAGEMENT MATRIX

IMPORTANT/URGENT (GET TO ASAP)
- Crises and emergencies (being locked out, stranded, or in any danger that can cause bodily harm, etc.).
- Pressing problems (needing to get a tooth pulled, needing to have a difficult conversation with your roommate).
- Deadlines (last-minute prep for a presentation or deadline).

IMPORTANT/NOT URGENT (GET SCHEDULED)
- Preparation and planning (needing to look up flights to travel home).
- Capability improvement (wanting to touch up your Spanish before the summer).
- Relationship building (needing to reach out and return calls or texts to new people you met over the weekend).
- Recreation/Relaxation (needing to book a nail appointment, read a book, or go to the gym).

	URGENT (GET TO ASAP)	**NOT URGENT** (GET SCHEDULED)
IMPORTANT		

NOT IMPORTANT/URGENT (GET TO AT SOME POINT)
- Interruptions (needing to call maintenance to have your closet door fixed).
- Calls and email (needing to respond to unread messages and clear notifications).
- Meetings/events (attending a floor social in the dorm).
- Popular activities (needing to rewrite your morning routine or organize your closet).

NOT URGENT/NOT IMPORTANT (GET RID OF)
- Busy work (needing to visit the new recreation center and other parts of campus).
- Trivial activities (wanting to remodel your dorm room with new decor purchased on Amazon).
- Time wasters (catching up on Netflix or binging the latest shows).
- Anything else that wastes time (scrolling on social media, procrastinating, etc.).

	URGENT BUT NOT IMPORTANT (GET TO AT SOME POINT)	**NOT URGENT AND NOT IMPORTANT** (GET RID OF)
NOT IMPORTANT		

Use this matrix or create your own and jot down your items!

	URGENT (GET TO ASAP)	**NOT URGENT** (GET SCHEDULED)
IMPORTANT		
NOT IMPORTANT	**URGENT BUT NOT IMPORTANT** (GET TO AT SOME POINT)	**NOT URGENT AND NOT IMPORTANT** (GET RID OF)

Do you know that one of the devil's greatest tactics is distraction and confusing urgent with important? If the devil can keep you distracted, procrastinating, full of anxiety, and confused about what requires your intention, then he can keep you further away from your calling, graduating, and being who God created you to be. The following time management matrix chart helps illustrate the breakdown of urgent vs. important regarding time management.

URGENT AND IMPORTANT

Do and eliminate these ASAP.

NOT URGENT BUT IMPORTANT

Most of your time will be spent here to get these items down.

URGENT BUT NOT IMPORTANT

Spend some time here but only a little.

NOT URGENT AND NOT IMPORTANT

Avoid and remove these items from your time allocation altogether.

You may have heard one of these phrases, "Time is money," "Time is expensive," or "Time is the one thing you can't get back." These are all true. The sooner you learn to manage your time more effectively, the sooner you'll have more of it. Time is so valuable in college and beyond, especially after graduation, because life seems to instantly speed up. While in college, learning to manage your time provides you with more of it. With good time management, you can complete your assignments on time, feel less stressed, be more productive, and even get your GPA up.

I encourage you to look ahead on your syllabus and always anticipate what's next to help you manage your time wisely. Time management is one of the hardest things to master, even for older adults. Admittedly, I still struggle with this sometimes because I like to knock things out as they arise. However, as you see in the quadrant example, everything doesn't need to be priority number one, and it can't be.

In college, you'll have your roommate who wants to hang out, other competing priorities, deadlines, family, and reading, and you'll need your own personal time. Getting clear about what needs to come first will save you so much time and energy. You'll also want to be aware of time thieves.

Remember I mentioned the devil wants nothing more than to distract you? He is also good at assigning people to your life with one specific goal: throwing you off focus. So pay attention to the people who always encourage you to do the opposite of what you say you need or want to do, especially if they are cosigning on wasting time.

With real friends, they will support you in handling your business because they want to see you win and be successful as well. Furthermore, like-minded friends are busy prioritizing their own business anyway. You must be very strict with your time because people who love to waste theirs will also help you waste yours.

Ladies, the days of winging it, waiting until the last minute, and Mama, Daddy, or your guardian telling you when to get up and what to do will be gone in college. You are in charge of setting the tone and handling business. While I occasionally struggle with prioritizing urgent vs. important, I understood time at an early age.

Growing up, I remember my grandpa telling me to walk like I had somewhere to be or like I had some business about myself. It also didn't help that my pet peeve as a high schooler and college student was lateness. Later, I had a career working in live television, where everything was down to the minute and second. I can't lie; eventually, I became a little too time conscious. You want to avoid this, too. You don't want to be too stringent on time when you're so focused on it that you can't enjoy what's before you because you're thinking about what you have to do next.

This is where the margin comes in. Margin, in the simplest way, is the additional time you leave for yourself to have breathing room. For example, if you went on a trip, you would take an extra day off from work on the back end of your trip, so you'll have it to decompress, unpack, and relax before returning to work. Or margin can be allowing yourself fifteen minutes before an interview to sit with material and get your mind right before walking in. Creating margin is valuable. When you manage your time well, you'll leave yourself enough margin to enjoy the moment, focus, get clear, and recuperate before hopping into the next thing.

> Now, let's break down some of these procrastination roots and discuss ways to remediate them.

Lack of Understanding/Intimidation

The best way to circumvent procrastination because you don't know or understand something is by making time for the learning curve. This is my root personally for when I procrastinate most. It happens when I don't know how to do something or if it will take too long to learn. However, with good time management, you can take tiny steps towards gaining an understanding and learning whatever is better.

When we know something and what we're talking about, we typically become less intimidated by it. Give this a shot, and just watch what happens to your confidence when you make the time to learn and gain understanding. You'll be fully equipped for whatever comes your way and find out that it actually wasn't that bad. It was just a matter of getting started.

Really Don't Want to Do It in the First Place
We procrastinate when we don't feel like doing something. A way to reduce this in life is not to make commitments or agree to things you can't keep or are not interested in. You'll have to be really honest with yourself. However, in college, when it comes to classwork, writing papers, or reading, no one wants to do any of this.

But doing what you don't want to do because you need to do it is called discipline, and discipline doesn't care how you feel. It's something you will have to suck up and do. Ask God to help you become more disciplined and take the steps by knocking out the stuff you don't want to do to build that muscle. Say no when you can and do what you can. Don't allow your laziness or disdain to win.

Lack of Respect
Procrastinating about something you need to do when you totally can and should do it communicates a lack of respect for the person asking you, a lack of respect for what's being asked of you, and a lack of respect for your time and the time of others. It sounds harsh, but disrespect is what it's giving, and it ain't cool. With this being said, you want to be mindful of your impression left on others and how this could potentially damage relationships.

It Will Require More

When a task or project feels overwhelming, and you assess that it will take way longer than you thought, procrastination keeps it there. This is why it's key to knock things out as they come or chip away at larger projects to save time and reduce anxiety associated with overwhelming tasks. Getting a full understanding can help you break it down into bite sizes and ask for help if needed.

Think about times when you procrastinated on cleaning your room because it felt like a lot. What if you started with simply making the bed, cleaning the dresser, sweeping the floor, and so on? The same goes for writing a paper. Break your task down into buckets. For example, you may want to read one night, write an outline the next night, start the intro and middle section, and leave the final parts and editing for the weekend. Do you see how the chip-away approach helps with this root of procrastination?

It's Too Easy

I know this sounds silly, but we often procrastinate most about all the small things, thinking, *it won't take long,* and *I will just do it later,* but later never comes, and all those small things you needed to do end up growing into something larger than life. Those tiny things can also trigger an entire meltdown, especially when you're overwhelmed.

For this root of procrastination, I like to use the 5x5 rule. This rule means if something can be knocked out in five minutes or less, please knock it out to free it off your plate. Those little things add up. So, if you have a single chapter to read or a one-page paper to write, please, by all means, knock it out!

MASTERING YOUR TIME IN COLLEGE

1. Get a full understanding of what's needed and what you have the capacity to commit to first.
2. List out and prioritize everything on your plate, using your urgent vs. important plan.
3. Try to reduce and avoid multitasking so you can focus and give your best to all your priorities.
4. Identify all distractions and eliminate them. Turn notifications off and utilize the DND on your phone.
5. Set boundaries, goals, and deadlines.
6. Complete the more challenging items when you have higher energy and feel good.

CHAPTER NINE

WOOSAH (BALANCE, STRESS MANAGEMENT, MENTAL HEALTH, AND HEALTHY HABITS

It isn't uncommon to experience a bit of sadness, isolation, and difficulty when adapting to the transition from high school to college. Balancing all the newness and freedom can be a lot. By the end of my third month away from home, freshman year, I was ready to drop out and give the military a shot. At that time, I had gotten into it with some girls on my floor and found out this guy I was talking to was seeing other people, there was drama back home, a friend from high school committed suicide, and it was an overall struggle to manage my social life.

Heaviness like this can easily alter your mental health and mood. I've been there more often than not, so topics like resilience, preventing burnout, stress, and mental health are near my heart.

Not only am I a career coach and strategist, but I also like to consider myself a workplace peace advocate. As college-bound students, school is your primary workplace and career for the next two to eight years, depending on your degree track. So, I'm here to be your workplace peace advocate and career strategist along your journey.

With the seriousness of this section in mind, I want to be sensitive, thoughtful, and practical as much as possible in delivering this chapter. Attending college will be your first time away from home and your first taste of independence for many of you. Even the thought of this can be overwhelming and anxiety-producing. But don't worry little sis, you will be fine, and you won't be alone. Here's something I know that can help keep you in a positive headspace: memorizing and building muscles to live out the Serenity Prayer. If you haven't heard of the Serenity Prayer, it goes like this:

God grant me the serenity to accept the things I cannot change, courage to change the things I can, and the wisdom to know the difference, living one day at a time; enjoying one moment at a time; taking this world as it is and not as I would have it; trusting that You will make all things right if I surrender to Your will; so that I may be reasonably happy in this life and supremely happy with You forever in the next. Amen.
—Reinhold Niebuhr[10]

You see, a prominent key to managing stress and mental health is using wisdom to know when you're at the end of you. And when you have done all you can do, meaning you have prepared, contributed, and showed up, the rest is up to God.

In life, we can get overwhelmed, stressed, depressed, burned out, and thrown off emotionally for many reasons, including being rejected, not setting boundaries, mismanaging priorities, experiencing the consequences of irresponsibility, worrying about things we can't change, taking on other

---

[10] Reinhold Niebuhr, "Prayer for Serenity," Celebrate Recovery, https://www.celebraterecovery.com/resources/serenity-prayer.

people's problems, and of course, tragedies and unexpected occurrences.

In this chapter, we will identify signs of burnout, and mental health issues, learn to manage stress, what self-care really means, how to establish boundaries, the value of being resilient, and strategies to keep you emotionally healthy and able to be your best in college and beyond. We want to always focus on the things we can change!

Your wellness is so important, and I'm talking about holistically. Holistic health covers every major wellness area, including financial, physical, spiritual, relational, and emotional wellness.

Each area of your wellness life helps to support and can impact another area. For example, if your bank account is low and you're feeling broke, that can cause stress, negatively impacting your mood. Your mood aligns with your emotional health. Here's another example. If you're off physically, you're less likely to have the energy to be social, and disengaging with friends can impact your relational wellness.

Do you see how they all align? My goal is to help you not only identify the importance of your wellness but also for you to be able to recognize when you're feeling off and to arm you with some tips for better managing stress, burnout, disappointment, and anything else that can negatively impact your mental and emotional health.

So first, let's explore a few definitions, the signs and symptoms of each, and how to manage them. We'll also dispel some myths associated with them as well.

DEPRESSION AND ANXIETY

I've noticed that depression and anxiety have been more popularized and publicly discussed in the last ten to fifteen years. These topics have become buzzwords and widely discussed even more after the pandemic. Previously, depression and mental health were taboo and unpopular to discuss in Black communities and culture for many reasons. Often, shame, ignorance, and isolation were displayed towards those whom Grandma or Big Mama referred to as "crazy," not knowing that term was derogatory itself. Mental health issues were not explored or respected, just written off as people being crazy.

Many of our elders and ancestors weren't encouraged to discuss their feelings or offered safe spaces to be heard or seen. They simply bottled their pain and unspeakable experiences up on the inside, exchanging silence for toxic masculinity and femininity. Yet the heaviness of their issues often reared its ugly head in unhealthy ways playing out at home.

For example, the Strong Black Woman is a toxic label, laced with pride and saturated in obligation. For centuries, Black women have been forced to lead, be strong, dominant, disrespected, and disregarded. Many of our mothers didn't show emotion, compassion, or empathy, thus reinforcing a nonverbal stoic "can do and I'll figure it out" persona that has caused more harm than good.

Yet here we are today, entering into and embracing a soft-girl era and movement, more accepting, aware, and sensitive to normalizing emotional pain, conversation, and ways to identify solutions as a culture. This is golden because we were not created to do life alone or in pain.

According to the American Psychological Association, anxiety is characterized by tension, worried thoughts, and physical changes, like increased blood pressure. The American Psychiatric Association defines depression as a serious medical illness that negatively affects how you feel, think and act.[11,12] There are also different types of depression as well. However, we don't have to get into those details for you to learn to identify when something is off, strategize, and implement sensible thinking.

HOW DEPRESSION AND ANXIETY MAY SHOW UP IN COLLEGE

Juggling classes, relationships, reading, being away from home, trying to fit in, managing time, and yearning for love and acceptance is absolutely normal when you get to college. You are not crazy, weird, worthless, or alone in this struggle, so please do not allow the devil to plant lies in your head that you are.

Yes, the devil is notorious for suggesting subtle thoughts and negativity to keep us off focus. He loves to make us think it's just us. But everyone you know is fighting a personal and internal battle you do not see, including your parents and those you admire.

Mental and emotional battles are just a part of life that will happen your entire life. However, these battles can be overcome and fought, every one of them. Below are some

---

[11] Adapted from the *Encyclopedia of Psychology* and APA Dictionary of Psychology, "Anxiety," American Psychological Association, https://www.apa.org/topics/anxiety.

[12] Felix Torres, M.D., MBA, DFAPA, "What Is Depression?" American Psychiatric Association, October 2020, https://www.psychiatry.org/patients-families/depression/what-is-depression.

specific examples of how depression and anxiety may show up while in college.

- Frequent unexplainable, negative emotions, including snapping at people, having a shorter temper, anger, sadness, and frustration.

- Not being able to sleep or eat, and constantly worrying something will happen or go wrong.

- Disinterest in things you usually like or in extracurricular activities, feeling nonchalant often and suddenly.

- Random guilt, shame, thinking things are pointless and stupid.

- Paranoia and overthinking about things that haven't and will likely never happen.

You, your roommate, or anyone you know may be experiencing the signs mentioned above at any given time. Therefore, I highly encourage you to pay attention to your own behaviors and those around you. Being empathetic and concerned can save a life—literally and figuratively.

STRATEGIES FOR OFFERING SUPPORT

1. Tell them you noticed something is off and remind them they are not alone. For example, "I noticed you haven't been eating or on the yard lately and a bit quieter than usual. I'm not sure what you're going through, but I'm here if you want to talk or need a sounding board."

2. Validate their feelings even if you don't understand or see things the same. Their feelings are theirs—not yours. For example, they tell you they have been feeling uninterested and overwhelmed with college. You can respond with, "I get it. I respect your feelings; they are real, and I've been there too, but I'm here for you, and we can get through this together."

3. Use wisdom, make sure you are listening and open, not overtalking, discrediting their feelings, or gauging how you would handle the situation. Be an ear and a voice of optimism. Don't be too pushy with trying to make anyone speak sooner than they would like. Treat them how you would want to be treated.

If you are experiencing some of these things yourself, please pray about them and pay attention to your emotions and thoughts. Also, please consider opening up and speaking with a trusted person. It isn't healthy or safe to be in your own head by yourself too long.

DEPRESSION, ANXIETY, AND ACCOUNTABILITY

Sometimes we are left to face consequences associated with our own poor decisions and improper planning. The consequences of our choices do not automatically warrant a depression diagnosis. This is where I have to be practical with you. For example, college students who do the following:

- Danielle spent her book money on clothing, thinking she could borrow books as needed. When she couldn't borrow books and fell behind on required reading, her grades dropped.

- Janea overdrafts her account, eating out weekly vs. in the café. She also chooses to get her hair/nails done instead of prioritizing bills, resulting in late rent and bill payments.

- Tierra enjoys being on the party scene and at every frat party vs. allowing enough study time. She's always crash reading and now has to drop classes because she's too behind to catch up. The dropped classes have impacted her financial aid, and she now faces probation.

These behaviors and consequences do not feel good and impact their mood and wellness. These ladies now claim to be depressed, although their choices were willful and self-inflicted. While they may feel depressed, this doesn't mean that they are. They're now left with the negative consequences of their behaviors. As you venture into the real world and become your own woman, learning to think and behave pragmatically, with resilience and responsibility, is crucial to success. Think about the examples above and know that feeling sadness, fear, or uncertainty in these cases does not mean you are depressed.

You may be feeling emotions associated with characteristics of depression for many different reasons, but again, this does not mean you have to claim depression. Knowing the difference between normal emotions, consequences triggering negative emotions, and actual medical illnesses is important.

Demonstrating healthy habits, integrity, awareness, and great character can help circumvent negative feelings. While feelings of depression can be triggered by things we do, don't do, and stress, there will be times when the roots are deeper, unidentifiable, or explainable. Times like these are when you want to seek professional help, especially if you can't pinpoint the cause of your mood shift.

Let's talk about some signs of burnout and stress.

BURNOUT AND STRESS

In short, burnout is a result of experiencing ongoing stress over a period of time. Specifically in college, things like getting acclimated to being away from home, heavy workloads, little finances, family issues, romantic relationships, drama with your roommate, and everything else can be stress-inducing. Without properly managing these stressors, they can lead to burnout.

Symptoms of burnout may include getting physically sick with headaches, fever blisters, fatigue, your brain feeling like it will explode, information overload, and high blood pressure. Nonphysical symptoms of burnout may include a lack of interest and motivation to do anything, detachment, apathy toward your academics, and irritability.

Students I've mentored or coached experienced burnout from poor time management (not prioritizing urgent over important), not thinking things through, neglecting their physical health, and a lack of organization. The biggest trend I've noticed with student burnout was stressing over things not in their control, setting unrealistic goals with high expectations, and having no plan or strategy to reach them.

Please know that life isn't going to stop or slow down to give you a moment to catch up. It will continue with or without you as well. This is why we discussed organization so much: creating margins, setting realistic goals, and time management. These are your keys to helping to avoid burnout and managing stress.

Granted, you've got to learn to let go of the things you can't control, do what you can, pray about it, and keep it moving.

I'll say this again for the people in the back: You've got to **really let go of what you can't control**. The hypotheticals, what-ifs, and I should haves will literally drive you insane too. Lastly, turning to alcohol, sex, tons of energy drinks, coffee, or drugs will not fix the roots and real issues that cause you stress. Learning to manage stress now will help you tremendously in the future.

STRESS MANAGEMENT TIPS

- Create a daily routine and get organized.

- List out what has you stressed and break it down into can change vs. can't change categories. Make a plan for what you can change.

- Take solid notes in class for references.

- Pace yourself with reading and break your work down into bite-size, taking breaks as needed.

- Don't procrastinate. Start early whenever you can, and pair up with others on top of their business.

- Think sensibly and be honest with yourself about your emotions; focus on what you can change.

- Move on quickly from mishaps and mistakes; do not punish or shame yourself. That moment is gone; don't get left behind.

- Manage your time like a pro.

- If you're struggling financially, think of ways to make money.

- Set healthy boundaries for yourself, eat well, implement self-care, and get some rest.

SELF-CARE AND BOUNDARY SETTING

Suppose you search the hashtag #selfcare on social media. In that case, you'll likely see images of people getting a mani/pedi or massage. While these are forms of self-care, I am challenging you ladies to think deeper. Self-care is more than doing things that pamper you. The short definition of self-care is establishing and enforcing boundaries for yourself. This section will cover boundaries and self-care because they are closely related.

Boundaries are invisible lines or rules that define what behaviors are acceptable and the things we won't tolerate from people. Maybe you haven't identified your boundaries yet. I get it because there will be times when we don't know them or have the words for our feelings until we later recognize when someone does something we don't like. The irritation we feel when people do things we don't like lets us know that a boundary has been crossed, even if we didn't know it existed.

When we know we aren't good, feel burned out, anxious, or stressed, these also indicate that boundaries were crossed. Because this happens too, the first thing you should do is identify your vulnerable areas. Vulnerable areas are things that bother or negatively impact you, revealing where you need boundaries.

Take a second and think through the vulnerable areas in your life that may need protecting. Think of stuff that bothers you and check out the examples following.

VULNERABLE AREAS THAT MAY NEED BOUNDARIES

- When friends talk over or interrupt you.

- Being cursed or yelled at or embarrassed.

- Being asked to borrow things all the time, run errands, or do things for others.

- Friends always dumping their problems on you but never ask how you're feeling or doing.

- Having your personal space invaded and being touched in ways you didn't agree to or don't like.

- People not apologizing to you when they were dead wrong.

- Friends being selfish towards you.

- Being asked a lot of personal information from others who don't share with you.

- When people try to drag you out to places, you don't want to be.

- Being around negative, gossiping, and draining personalities.

Putting boundaries in place for our vulnerable areas is the highest form of self-care to protect our peace and holistic wellness. A more comprehensive definition of self-care is identifying your needs, vocalizing them, and advocating for yourself until those needs are met.

Imagine being in charge of a baby sibling under a year old. Wouldn't you need to cherish, feed, protect, love, and care for the child? YES! Similarly, you've got to see yourself as your own baby, who needs that same love, care, attention, and protection, including from yourself at times.

As humans, we all have core and similar needs because God created us that way. You may need to feel a deeper sense of love, affection, attention, identity, purpose, and value at your age. These are all normal but can become a problem when we seek to get these needs met in unhealthy ways or allow others seeking the same to trample over us.

Consequently, this is why I define self-care as deciding what you need and ensuring that need is met. Notice, I said *need* and not *want*. Needs align more with the essentials you must have to live, supporting our wellness areas. Wants are things we desire, BTW. Think of self-care as getting what you need. I've included examples below to get your brain thinking.

Be sure to add your own ideas.

Example:
I need <u>more sleep</u>, so I will <u>get to bed earlier</u> and make sure this happens by <u>setting a reminder on my phone to shut things down earlier</u>.

Your turn:

I need _____, so I will _____ and make sure this happens by _____.

VALUES
1. My peace.
2. My friendships.
3. Clarity and focus.

NEEDS
1. Eliminate toxicity.
2. Check on my friends more often.
3. Spend more time meditating.

ACTION PLAN
1. Restrict what I watch and who I hang with.
2. Be intentional with responding to texts and calls.
3. Create and stick to a morning routine.

Based on your vulnerable areas and needs, think about what boundaries you can put in place and ways to stick to them to avoid feeling slighted. The following are examples of vulnerable areas with boundary talking points and recommended actions.

WOOSAH

THE PROBLEM (VULNERABLE AREA)
- When friends talk over or interrupt you.

WHAT TO SAY (BOUNDARY TALKING POINT)
- "Hey friend, I would like to get my complete thought out and finish my sentence before you chime in."

WHAT TO DO (RECOMMENDED ACTION)
- End the conversation if they don't stop.

THE PROBLEM (VULNERABLE AREA)
- Friends always dumping their problems on you but never asking how you're feeling or doing.

WHAT TO SAY (BOUNDARY TALKING POINT)
- "Hey sis, I understand you have a lot going on and I want to be here for you, but I have a lot going on too, and I just don't have the capacity for both our drama."

WHAT TO DO (RECOMMENDED ACTION)
- Change the conversation or redirect it to something positive when you feel it going downhill.

COLLEGE BOUND: A BLACK GIRL'S GUIDE

SETTING BOUNDARIES FOR YOURSELF

THE PROBLEMS
- Binge-watching shows. Wasting study time.
- Social media distractions.
- Overeating or eating poorly.
- Staying out too late.

THE BOUNDARY
- Limit yourself to two hours a day or earn watching a show after your work is done.
- Download an app that restricts your access, deactivates your accounts, or have your friends change your passwords and only give them back after midterms or exams.
- Track your calories. Don't buy sweets and fatty foods.
- Give yourself a curfew.

Boundaries also help to protect us and ensure our needs are met. Boundaries for every area of our lives should be established. For students, many of your boundary needs may be relational. We talked about the importance of self-care and how this relates to boundaries. I'm hoping you better understand the value and importance of getting what you need. Implementing healthy self-care in college and beyond is a key to reducing burnout, depression, and stress.

Let's look at different forms of self-care.

FORMS OF SELF-CARE

1. Taking a setback to evaluate your relationships, including with family and close friends. Pinpointing who your drains and faucets are.

2. Reflecting on how you're doing. Clapping for what you've accomplished and learning from your losses.

3. Forgiving and not shaming yourself. No negative self-talk.

4. Asking for help and allowing others to help you.

5. Speaking up, defending yourself, and asking for what you need.

6. Being quiet at times, knowing you don't have to prove yourself.

7. Setting boundaries and saying no.

8. Laughing.

9. Looking and feeling good.

10. Being accountable.

I want to close this chapter by discussing what resilience means and why it's necessary for your life. Resilience speaks to having the ability to endure or recover quickly from challenges, difficulties, and hard times. I know you heard the phrase "keep it moving" or one of the many motivational choruses in a Beyonce song. There is power in being resilient. For young

Black girls, it's in our DNA and one of our secret weapons to success.

Earlier, I mentioned that life will always continue with or without you. This is true, and it's also true that life will be filled with trials, ups and downs, and lots of change. Change is one constant that you will experience for the rest of your life. Change can be hard for some and easier for others.

With change comes the importance of being resilient. If you can tell yourself this now and truly get it in your head, the reality that you will experience change and challenges, you can subconsciously prepare yourself to be resilient. Here's a sample chart of how to encourage and practice resilience at your age.

RESILIENT WOMEN

Do the following:

- Have a willingness to communicate and overcome challenges rather than run from them
- Keep a high self- esteem
- Stay positive and optimistic
- Set realistic goals and expectations
- Practice emotional intelligence
- Sharpen their social skills
- Practice healthy coping strategies
- Demonstrate self-control
- Understand and accept weaknesses and strengths
- Implement self-care
- Learn from their mistakes
- Practice problem-solving skills
- Connect with their school and community

7 TIPS FOR BEING RESILIENT IN COLLEGE

1. Be proactive and assess situations fully, anticipating what could go wrong in a healthy and realistic way.

2. Think through possible contingencies, but don't dwell on them (realism and optimism can coexist).

3. Stay focused on the real thing, not the distraction. Keep things in perspective.

4. Know that this moment will pass, and trouble doesn't last forever.

5. Build healthy relationships, asking for and accepting help and support when needed.

6. Practice gratitude and focus on what you can control.

7. Leverage your strengths.

CHAPTER TEN
RELATIONSHIP MANAGEMENT, COMMUNICATING, AND RESOLVING CONFLICT

It was the spring of 2007, and I was in the final stretch of my undergrad program at Texas Southern, preparing to host a graduation party, land my first job, and enter the real world. Some of the most profound advice I ever heard came to me that same semester, packaged in words of wisdom from my advisor and one of my rambunctious uncles.

My advisor said, "It's who you know that will get you in the door, and what you know will keep you there." Meanwhile, deciding between chicken or beef for the graduation party, my uncle affectionately blurted out, "Well, Rahk, you can't please everyone." Both phrases have guided my approach to networking, building, and maintaining relationships ever since.

Over the years, I learned just how important relationships are, and over the last five years, I've outgrown many. Relationships are everything and a vital component to the outcome of our success. Until you die, you will always be in a community/relationship with someone unless you're completely isolated on an island. Even then, you may need someone to talk to or to bring you food. LOL.

Speaking of isolation, it always amazes me when I hear people say, "They don't need anyone," or when I hear women say, "They don't do women." This is often said in reference to the fear of experiencing cattiness and girl drama. There are plenty of stigmas around making new girlfriends, so I kind of get it. However, these statements are not only prideful but also immature, and having this attitude can block your blessings. Did you know that many of life's greatest lessons and blessings are generated through being in relationships with other people? Absolutely no one got to where they are in life without someone else's support.

The same is true for you. Many of the connections you'll make in college will be people you do life with. At least, this was the case for me and almost everyone I know who attended college. People have met their husbands, and future bosses, and even sat alongside future local politicians and news reporters. Personally, I've had the privilege of making long-lasting connections with people from college who have afforded me jobs, opportunities to travel, and wonderful friendships.

Every relationship may not blossom into a friendship, and that's perfectly fine. I do believe relationships should be grouped into categories with equal respect to their appropriate category. However, the relationships that you hold dear should be cherished, protected, and nurtured.

Building relationships should be intentional and strategic. They should also be a two-way street and not only transactional unless they call for this.

The first thing I would encourage you to do when building relationships is to observe people's behaviors and discern their motives and intentions. I don't think I need to tell you this but stay away from gossipers, pessimists, and loud and messy people. If someone easily talks about others in their absence, they will also talk about you. You can always be cordial, warm, and friendly, but this doesn't automatically guarantee you'll be friends.

I learned the hard way that just because you place and view someone in high esteem doesn't mean they will see you the same. It is possible to consider someone an associate. Meanwhile, they're considering you a best friend. Sounds weird, right? That speaks to values, and everyone values different things. Let's dive into a couple of relationship types, followed by strategies for navigating conflict, making and maintaining relationships, and how to heal from losing friends or breakups.

RELATIONSHIP TYPES

- **Romantic Relationships.** You are involved with these people on a more intimate and personal level. People you are dating or have dated. Some of these can shift into other categories, but once that line is crossed, this can be more challenging, especially if you or the other party isn't mature enough to look beyond the breakup.

- **Homies.** This can be people who you kick it with. They are generally down with you, and for you in the moment you're together, but they are typically not who you confide in or call when things really hit the fan.

- **Friends.** This is a level up from a homie, as this person is dependable. Although y'all may not speak or hang on a regular at all, they would be there if you needed them or anything.

- **Bestie.** This person is a solid friend but one who knows all your dirty laundry and junk for the most part. They are also loyal, and y'all are in some form of communication daily, every other day, or at least five times a week.

- **Squad.** This person is a part of the hang-out crew. You may not know each other personally and deeply, but they are kind of like homies but in a group. The difference between a squad and a homie is that you and the homie may hang one-on-one, but you and the squad members usually only hang with the entire squad.

- **Acquaintance/Familiar.** These are people you see regularly at the gym, church, or in class, and y'all speak and have small talk when you connect.

- **Formal Acquaintances.** These people are acquaintances/familiar people you may see often and speak to. You might even struggle to remember their name, but you know their face.

The relationship categories mentioned above are examples, not the end all, be all. Please feel free to add your own. Those categories are based on a few of my experiences over the years.

Remember how easy it was to make friends and build relationships in middle school? But now, the process has changed quite a bit. Life has a funny way of repeatedly presenting the same or similar things, like making friends at different stages. While many situations are the same, we are the only ones that actually change. Hopefully, changing for the better and becoming wiser.

RELATIONSHIP MANAGEMENT, COMMUNICATING, AND RESOLVING CONFLICT

Making friends at the college level can help you navigate all the new changes in life by providing a support system and making college more enjoyable. Think of those same friends from middle school and high school. School wouldn't have been the same without them, right? But everyone didn't make it to your inner circle either.

I learned the importance of knowing where to place people after learning why they needed to be placed in the first place. You've got to place people in categories to help reduce disappointment and to create a boundary of where you stand with them. Knowing where you stand helps create a more accurate expectation of that relationship, allowing you to act accordingly. Everyone isn't your friend, and the friendship title must be earned. Because friendship comes with responsibility, it's not to be taken lightly.

A friend is someone who is not only loyal and nonjudgmental but also selfless, consistent, and kind. Typically, you don't have to question their allegiance or heart. However, people do change and also outgrow each other. This happens when someone isn't challenging themselves, choosing to stay stagnant, or refusing to embrace change.

You may not see this at first at the start of most friendships. However, as you start to notice a change in values, misalignment in interests, and how things are handled, someone is usually outgrowing the other.

In most cases, when you begin to outgrow relationships, it can be uncomfortable, especially if this is someone you were really close to. Outgrowing friends does not mean you're beefing or that it has to get ugly. If they are worth keeping in your life, you may need to shift their category and revoke some of their personal access to you.

Sidenote: You are not obligated to stay in relationships with people just because you've known them since third grade.

Third grade may have been their mission and assignment in your life, and that's it. Often, we allow people to stay much longer in our lives than we should and don't know this until there is conflict.

LET'S TALK ABOUT CONFLICT

There will always be conflict in most relationships, including with family, on the job, and with friends. Conflict isn't a bad thing if it's healthy. Healthy conflict is important for many reasons. While uncomfortable, healthy conflict brings issues to the surface, providing an opportunity for healing (if you're both mature and willing to communicate). At the same time, conflict and misunderstandings will also reveal where you stand with people, their true motives, and perceptions about you.

If the relationship is worth investing in and keeping, consider the following steps to engage in healthy conflict. Please know that you may not and will not be able to resolve conflict with everyone. Some people are too defensive and immature to communicate. If you've asked or initiated a conversation and they refuse, don't waste your time or energy on these people. Pray for them and keep it moving.

RELATIONSHIP MANAGEMENT, COMMUNICATING, AND RESOLVING CONFLICT

7 CONFLICT RESOLUTION TIPS FOR COLLEGE STUDENTS

COOL OFF FIRST
Do not go to social media announcing what happened or sub-mention anyone.

PROCESS THE REAL PROBLEM
Do this by yourself! Think about why you are offended. Do you feel played, betrayed, or hurt, and why?

ASK TO ENGAGE
In conversation, let them know you want to get some clarity, share a few things, and hear their heart/perspective on some things, too. Please don't do this on social media or via text. This needs to be a face-to-face request.

BE ACCOUNTABLE
Take responsibility for areas they have brought to your attention that are fair. If you don't agree or see it as such, you can still validate their feelings but express that you don't agree with them.

COLLECTIVELY TALK
Talk through solutions to move forward and decide which solution you will agree on.

LISTEN TO HEAR
Share, listen to hear and not to respond, and check to make sure there is an understanding that you both heard each other, and that real communication took place.

END WELL
End the conversation by acknowledging what happened, apologizing or forgiving, reiterating solutions, and thanking them for having the conversation. Keep what you discussed between the two of you.

CONFLICT WITH ROOMMATES

Conflict resolution with roommates can be tricky and requires a different approach. This becomes tricky because the conflict is now in your place of residence, your room, and the place you call home.

Most conflicts with roommates start with a lack of communication or miscommunication. Conflict with roommates can stem from different reasons, including different cleaning and hygiene practices, a lack of respect for personal space, stuff, and study time, being too loud, different values, jealousy, and flat-out selfishness. They say you really don't know someone until you live with them, and that couldn't be any truer. Even if you knew your roomie from high school, you still don't really know them until you can observe them day in and day out.

Living together takes relationships to another level, requiring trust and a deeper respect. When first connecting

RELATIONSHIP MANAGEMENT, COMMUNICATING, AND RESOLVING CONFLICT

with a roommate, I recommend getting to know them, sharing a bit about yourself, and establishing house and ground rules together that first week. Granted, one or both of you may fall off the wagon, but at least you will have them in place to refer to if you need to level-set.

You may be more mature than your roommate and open to communication and conflict resolution, so watch out for this. If you notice shady behaviors, don't ignore them. You will need to exercise your maturity and initiate a conversation using the strategies previously mentioned and the ones below. I know you may not want to, but building this communication muscle will make you a much better woman.

Some people are too defensive and immature to communicate. Don't waste your time or energy if you've asked them to talk or tried to initiate a conversation and they refuse. Consider getting your resident assistant or dorm leader involved. You can also request to be moved.

SAMPLE GROUND RULES FOR ROOMMATE LIVING

- Agree on a quiet/lights-out time and consider contingencies if someone needs to study late. For example, consider getting an eye mask.

- Agree on cleaning schedules, cleaning expectations, and nonnegotiables. For example, hair in the sink, dirty mirrors, leaving clothing on the floor, and wet floors (if you have a bathroom in your room).

- Ask before touching/borrowing each other's stuff.

- Agree on the types and frequency of company that will come over.

- Agree to mutually respect and communicate with each other when there are issues (in person). Consider having a monthly or weekly check-in.

HOW TO TELL IF YOUR ROOMMATE HAS A PROBLEM

- They begin acting funny: not talking to you, being really brief, avoiding you, staying gone for long periods, talking about you.

- They don't intentionally adhere to your ground rules and easily become annoyed with you.

- They begin to indirectly share issues about you on social media.

HOW TO RESOLVE CONFLICT WITH ROOMMATES

- First things first, follow all the steps listed above (start with a cool down and think about what you want to address).

- Approach them privately and ask if you can converse with them (face-to-face). Identify the best time for both of you to speak. If someone feels rushed, ambushed, or reads this via text, it can be misinterpreted and may not go well.

- Because you've processed your thoughts, be direct and get to the point. Stick to the issue and don't focus on their personality, things that annoy you, or how or why they did something. Focus on what the problem is.

RELATIONSHIP MANAGEMENT, COMMUNICATING, AND RESOLVING CONFLICT

- Proceed with the other conflict resolution steps: Share, listen to hear and not to respond, and check to make sure there is an understanding. Be accountable and take responsibility. Collectively talk through solutions, agree on one, end the conversation by acknowledging what happened, apologize or forgive, reiterate the solution, and thank them for having the conversation. Keep what you discussed between the two of you.

BEST PRACTICES FOR COMMUNICATION

- Be real with yourself when something is bothering you, or a boundary has been crossed. Process what you are feeling. Think about what you hope to accomplish in the conversation and share your intention when you begin.

- Discern and locate an appropriate time to have a conversation, especially sensitive ones. If someone just got an F on an exam or got bad news from home, that may not be a smart time to engage in a heartfelt conversation.

- Communicate directly with your friends, roommate, or whomever when something bothers you (using the abovementioned strategies). Don't beat around the bush. There is a high possibility that they are unaware of their behavior or if something bothers you.

- Don't get on social media or talk about issues behind people's backs before speaking directly with them. This can break trust, and it's messy. If you're looking for advice and feedback on approaching a situation, consider speaking with someone older, unbiased, or who does not know the people you are talking about.

- Remember that communication is a two-way street that requires talking and listening, and the person may have an opinion or see issues differently than you. It's perfectly fine to agree to disagree but to still validate someone's feelings.

- Don't interrupt or be sarcastic during serious situations and conversations. Even if you don't agree, you can still make them feel heard.

- Remember, you both may have needs, and coming to a compromise is the best way to get needs met.

- Respect each other's differences and consider the person's heart vs. the delivery, especially if you have a good rapport with them. Based on everyone's different backgrounds and communication styles, the delivery may come across not as intended, especially if they talk loudly. Always be open and get clarity when needed.

- Consider having a wise and responsible mediator if the conversation gets too heated.

Your relationships, and friends especially, are the most influential in your life. Having solid communication skills and being connected to either high-quality or poor-quality people in college can hinder or add greatly to your life and college career. So, always take a mature approach and choose wisely moving forward.

RELATIONSHIP MANAGEMENT, COMMUNICATING, AND RESOLVING CONFLICT

TIPS FOR MAKING FRIENDS

I hope you're not feeling too overwhelmed by all of this information. Little sis, it's time to put on your big girl panties and to grow. I promise the more you can practice these strategies now, the better woman you will be. I learned much of this stuff way later in life and sometimes wonder how different things could have gone if I had this knowledge. So, baby girl, there are no excuses. You know what to do with conflict and the value of relationships.

Perhaps you're a commuter student, a transfer student, or an introvert. The awkwardness and vulnerability it takes to get to know new people is real. All fair concerns. However, genuinely and authentically putting yourself out there is what you have to do. The rest will organically take care of itself. What's for you is for you; you won't have to force it, and you won't be for everyone, and that's okay.

When making friends, be mindful not to rush into calling people you hardly know your BFF. Also, don't be super guarded that you miss out on a connection. Pay attention to what people say, how they carry themselves, their energy, and what they do. People will tell you everything you need to know about themselves if you're listening, including the nonverbals.

You can also make a personal commitment to being the type of friend that you want. Making new friends can be challenging the older you get, but it's worth it, especially in college. Being in a community with like-minded and similarly focused people is great for your mental health. A great friend is more valuable than gold! Ahead are a couple of tips for making friends in college. Make sure you remain open, observant, and authentic. You got this!

MAKING FRIENDS IN COLLEGE

1. **Compliment** others you see that are doing their thing. A compliment doesn't hurt or take anything away from you.

2. **Be friendly**, approachable, and the type of friend you want to meet.

3. **Engage** with classmates and in class discussions and speak to people you see. Ask their names and call them by name so they feel valued and build a personal connection.

4. **Join study groups** or create them, and study with others when you can.

5. **Be visible** on the yard, quad, or popular gathering areas.

6. **Attend parties**, networking/sporting events, and anything on campus. Don't be afraid to walk up and join others in the café.

7. **Join organizations** on campus.

8. **Connect** with and follow people from your school on socials or LinkedIn.

STRATEGIES FOR MAINTAINING RELATIONSHIPS

Earlier, I used the phrase transactional relationships and wanted to circle back to this. A transactional relationship is one where you only engage when you need something. They are usually mutually beneficial and kind of like a scratch my back, and I'll scratch yours. While transactional relationships do have their own place (usually in the business world), your closest friends and loved ones do not want to feel transactional.

Think about it. You can't say you're super enthusiastic when your phone rings from people who only hit you up when they want or need something. No one likes to feel used, and contrary to popular belief, our relationships are not just about us. You may be more talkative, dramatic, emotional, or turn up than some of your friends, but that doesn't mean they don't have things going on or things they want to discuss, especially if they can't get a word in.

Perhaps you're on the other end of the spectrum, really chill, and the quiet friend. You still have thoughts and an opinion, too, and your friends would love to know what's on your mind if you're willing to share.

All this to say, as a friend or active participant in any relationship, it will be important to do your part to help maintain it. And even if you still feel you need more from the other person in the relationship after doing your part, have an open dialogue.

The following are some examples of healthy relationships and ways to maintain them. The information is just as applicable if you are in a dating relationship. Remember, your mental and social wellness is so important, so do your part to keep these intact.

TRAITS OF TOXIC RELATIONSHIPS
- ☑ Gaslighting (emotional manipulation)
- ☑ Abuse (physical, verbal, or mental)
- ☑ Jealousy
- ☑ Dishonesty
- ☑ Insecurity
- ☑ Narcissism
- ☑ Selfishness
- ☑ Fear tactics and intimidation

TRAITS OF HEALTHY RELATIONSHIPS
- ☑ Trust
- ☑ Honesty
- ☑ Safety
- ☑ Security
- ☑ Support
- ☑ Protection
- ☑ Love
- ☑ Patience and kindness
- ☑ Forgiveness
- ☑ Healthy communication

HOW TO MAINTAIN RELATIONSHIPS
- ☑ Offer a helpful hand.
- ☑ Be supportive and considerate.
- ☑ Check on others and demonstrate care.
- ☑ Affirm your relationships and those in them.
- ☑ Call to let them know you're thinking of them.
- ☑ Give birthday or holiday gifts and cards.
- ☑ Recommend them for opportunities.
- ☑ Acknowledge when they are working hard.
- ☑ Listen and don't judge them.

HEALING FROM BREAKUPS
(ROMANTIC AND PLATONIC)

There is an old adage that says some people are in our lives for reasons, some seasons, and some lifetimes. Knowing when someone's time or season is up can be hard to gauge. Whether you physically lost a loved one or had a nasty falling out, a slow drift to ghosting, or a hard breakup, separating from a dear relationship hurts all the same.

No one wants to feel like they've lost, especially not someone they care about and will miss. The acceptance and moving beyond phase is rough but temporary. I can't say that time actually heals all, but I do know that with time, it gets easier to manage, and some breakups do become forgotten memories.

Have you ever taken a moment to ask yourself or think through how you deal with loss, hurt, and disappointment? Your answer may reveal a possible growth gap or area that needs attention. Seriously, think about your response for a second. While this section deals with relationship losses, pain and disappointment feels like pain and disappointment, even if it's a job loss.

If you can learn to develop healthy breakup coping skills at your age, you will be tremendously prepared for the future. I'm referring to all types of relationships and breakups—not just romantic ones.

In life, you will experience loss and disappointment for sure. One of the most helpful things you can do in your healing process is to separate what you feel from who you are. For example, process your hurt and sadness. Tell yourself you feel hurt or sad vs. embodying those emotions. Sadness and hurt are emotion-based feelings that will eventually pass. Therefore, you have to avoid taking these on as character traits.

Being in your feelings too long, acting off emotion, and thinking illogically can get you in big trouble. I like to tell people this. *Your feelings will take you on a whole trip and leave you stranded.* Your feelings are fickle and unreliable. You can acknowledge and feel them but don't sit with them too long or allow them to drive your actions.

Forgiveness is also a critical part of healing. I know that forgiveness is tough, but forgiving gives you more peace and the ability to heal. If the relationship ended because of you, be sure to forgive yourself and the other person. I'm assuming you did the best you could based on what you knew to do at that time, but you've grown now.

I can't even lie; forgiveness isn't easy. It's supernatural, which means God will have to help you with this. You'll have to pray and ask Him to help you forgive and remove any hate from your heart so you can move on. You may even need to keep praying this prayer often, especially if you have class with or see the person you're struggling to forgive often.

You will also have to release any guilt associated with what you wish you did or thinking something is wrong with you specifically. There is nothing wrong with you. You are a human who deserves to move on with her life. And, if the other person you were beefing with is at fault, their actions have nothing to do with you. Please do not take responsibility for someone else's actions. This does not reflect you, PERIOD.

Lastly, please evaluate what you could have done differently as you process. This is your opportunity to turn that L (loss) into another type of L (lesson). After you've processed what you've learned, consider how you can apply that wisdom to current relationships.

Possible lessons learned can include:

- Identifying if you see a pattern in the type of people you attract, hang with, or are attracted to.

- Were you allowing people to be themselves, or were you trying to have them be something you wanted them to be?

- What role did you play in the breakup of the relationship?

- Did you initiate or try to engage in healthy communication?

Breakups in college can feel like the end of the world and cause much rejection, isolation, and even insecurity, but you are a resilient woman, and you will grow through this. Every heartbreak produces an opportunity for growth.

Hey, you never know. Some breakups may bring you the peace you didn't know you needed. Don't be afraid to trust, love, and put yourself out there again.

TIPS TO HEAL FROM BREAKUPS AND RELATIONSHIP LOSS IN COLLEGE

- Know that there is nothing wrong with you.

- Remember, it is not the end of the world, and you have so much new and exciting life ahead.

- Put your energy into working out or reading/learning.

- Feel free to block and remove ex-friends from social media.

- Discover your interests and find new hobbies and outlets.

- Process your feelings and look for ways to revamp your other relationships.

- Set new standards for what you want in your life.

- Implement self-care, get to know **you** more, and love on yourself like never before.

- Pray and spend time with God.

- Enjoy what you do have and your other friends by practicing gratitude.

- Avoid unhealthy coping mechanisms like overeating, drugs, sex, and alcohol.

 WAYS TO HAVE A BETTER RELATIONSHIP WITH YOURSELF

1. Spend time with God.
2. Be kind, patient, and gracious to yourself.
3. Remember that you are learning and a work in progress.
4. No negative self-talk.
5. Journal and implement self-care (identifying and expressing your needs).
6. Take care of your holistic wellness (body, mind, spirit).
7. Make sure your cup is full before you pour out for others.
8. Unplug and make intentional time for yourself

CHAPTER ELEVEN

NAVIGATING CAMPUS, THE SOCIAL SCENE, AND GOING HOME

This chapter will discuss a few things, from navigating your campus, joining organizations, safety tips, and returning home. Please note that everything I share is just a rule of thumb, and every campus and college experience differs. What may be easy-peasy or obvious for you may be terrifying or new for someone else, and vice versa. Let's start with the most important thing: safety.

Did you know that in the United States, nearly 100,000 women of color went missing in 2020? And according to an article composed in *TheGrio* in early 2023, although only 13 percent of the female population here in the U.S., Black women account for over 30 percent of the country's missing women.[13]

Not only is this terrifying, but also startling. Missing Black women and girls do not get nearly the same media coverage as missing white women and girls. The problem with this is that the chances of these women being found are slim without media coverage.

---

[13] TheGrio Staff, "Nearly 100,000 women of color went missing in 2020, and now one state wants to do something about it," thegrio, Mar. 3, 2023, https://thegrio.com/2023/03/03/minnesota-first-office-missing-murdered-black-women-girls/.

It is also reported that Black women are twice as likely to be homicide victims and are involved in missing cases that remain open for four times as long as cases for white individuals. It is believed that sex trafficking, mental health, and domestic violence issues are at the root of these women going missing.

Some studies show Black women are disproportionately at risk for sexual assault. For every Black woman who reports rape, at least fifteen do not report their assaults. Shame, guilt, fear of being retaliated against, fear of not being believed, not wanting negative attention, and protecting their assailant are among the top reasons why women aren't speaking up.[14]

Ladies, your safety must be prioritized and taken seriously—always. You deserve to be loved, protected, and safe!

What does this mean for you in college? While much of your life will be spent on a college campus or commuting (if you're not on campus), you are not exempted from assault and kidnapping. So please be aware of your surroundings, vigilant, and always practice safe habits.

Pray for protection and trust your gut. Stay in the know of new sex-trafficking tactics and what's happening in the news around you, even if you're browsing headlines here and there. A simple act of staying knowledgeable and aware can help to save your life. People are becoming more bold, clever, and crazier these days, assaulting and kidnapping women.

---

[14] NBWJI, "Black Women, Sexual Assault, and Criminalization," National Black Women's Justice Institute, Apr. 11, https://www.nbwji.org/post/black-women-sexual-assault-criminalization.

SAFETY TIPS FOR WOMEN IN COLLEGE

- Do not share your location on social media. If shared, restrict sharing to only trusted friends.

- Be mindful of walking with earbuds, AirPods, or headphones on campus when going to the store or when you're solo.

- Reduce trips at night by yourself.

- Make a habit of looking behind you, watching your surroundings, and paying attention to others in your vicinity.

- Don't give people your phone, take things from strangers, or smell random scents when being offered. Women are being drugged daily, kidnapped in clever ways, and held as sex slaves.

- Lock your doors all the time.

- No buzz driving or riding with buzzed drivers.

- Reduce distractions altogether, including being on the phone while commuting, pumping gas, or walking into places.

- When meeting people online, whether dating apps or marketplace purchases, have someone come with you, screenshot profiles of who you're meeting, and share them with a trusted friend.

- When meeting up with new people, always text a friend the address, their license plate, and name.

- Do not leave your cups or food unattended.

- If there is something weird on your car or door handles, don't touch it with your hands.

- Meet all food delivery persons in the dorm lobby or public spaces, and Uber or Lyft drivers in public spaces as well.

- Consider taking self-defense classes, carrying mace, or getting a Taser.

- Don't attend parties or clubs solo, and when meeting up with friends, meet in lit/public places.

- If you experience assault, please speak up and use your voice to help prevent this from happening to another woman.

- As an extra precaution, you can also google, check social media profiles, and intentionally vet guys you meet.

THE YARD/QUAD/CAMPUS AND SOCIAL SCENE

Ah, the parties, the yard/campus, and the excitement of college living outside of reading completing assignments, crash studying, and writing papers. College can be loads of fun, wonder, and a special taste of independent living. It can also be a wonderful space to cultivate a new identity, mature, and to lay the foundations for an exciting career. However, there is also a dark side to navigating college living. That side includes getting caught up in the hype of freedom, overindulging, and lacking discipline, self-control, and focus.

Students without a deep sense of self who gravitate to the hype of clout chasing, reckless behaviors, and doing too much are the ones who don't return the second semester. They often drop out, get pregnant, contract sexually transmitted diseases, go into debt, have depression, and have downward spirals. This doesn't mean that hope is lost for them. However, we don't want this to be your story.

The keys to enjoying life as a college student navigating the campus and social scene are moderation and consideration. Consider the boundaries you've set for yourself; consider how your decisions may impact you or your family. Consider your studies, your future, and the reason you're in school in the first place. Enjoy what college has to offer in moderation, demonstrating self-control. Commit to implementing everything you've learned in previous chapters to help ensure success.

1. Don't try too hard or aim to be someone you're not.

2. People do talk and always will, so carry yourself in ways you don't mind being talked about.

3. Everyone ain't your friend, so choose friends and your squad wisely. You want people who are not only cool but who can also add value to your life.

4. Don't be that girl at every party or always on the scene. Have a little mystery about yourself.

5. Get involved, join clubs, and make a name for yourself in your department and with your professors and advisors.

6. If you need help with something, please ask! Don't be too proud.

7. Don't compromise or negotiate with yourself.

8. Set boundaries and enforce them.

9. Stay organized and on top of your studies.

10. Always apply for scholarships, keep your GPA up, intern, volunteer, and prepare for life after college. College will be what you make it.

ORGANIZATIONS, CLUBS, AND GREEK LIFE

Being connected and a part of a mission or cause greater than yourself can be exciting and fulfilling. In college specifically, joining organizations and clubs helps you not only gain new skills and make friends, but they also can provide a sense of purpose, popularity, and belonging.

Most campuses are filled with clubs, fraternities, sororities, and various organizations. There is usually something for everyone; if you don't see something you're interested in, you can always start your own thing. Unlike high school, you have full autonomy to join as many clubs and organizations as you want. However, I must caution you to always keep in mind your purpose of being in school in the first place and your identity outside of the club or organization.

There is always a good and potential dark side to everything. Let's talk about some options you may have on campus and their pros and cons. Remember that every school is different, and the list I'll share isn't final or applicable to every campus. You may not have many options if you are at a community college or a smaller university.

ORGANIZATION TYPES
Academic and educational
Community service
Media and publication
Political or multicultural
Recreation and sports
Student government
Religious and spiritual

ORGANIZATION EXAMPLES
The Honor Society or Psi Chi and Psychology Club
Black fraternities and sororities
Journalism or film clubs
Black Student Union/International Students Association (ISA)
Majorettes, dance clubs, sports teams, etc.
Student government or councils
Campus Crusade for Christ, or Baptist Student Union

Identifying organizations aligning with your mission, faith, career aspirations, and values can be a smart and strategic move for the future, especially if you plug into clubs that represent your major and career field. This allows you an opportunity to network and build with potential future colleagues.

When considering what organization to join, especially if it is a fraternity or sorority, make sure you are being very smart and strategic with your research. Aim to learn the policies of governing bodies and what may be required of you upfront.

Speaking of Greek life, I know for many of you, learning more about frats and sororities is the highlight of this book. LOL. For many girls, going to college is usually associated with pledging and being a part of a sorority. Either they had parents, an aunt, a teacher, or a woman in their life who was a part of an organization that left an impression on them.

For the record, I am not a member of any Greek organizations and currently have no interest in joining one (yes, you can still join them after college at any time). I reference this to let you know that my feelings towards them are equal, and I am not partial to any.

Let's dive into a little information about Greek organizations. If you're considering joining one, I want to ask some questions to get you thinking of your why.

Greek Life encompasses fraternities and sororities overall. Moving forward, I will only reference sororities, as this book is for girls. However, for Black sororities, many of the focus and practices differ from white sororities. There is a wealth of information available on the internet to expound more on this. Please do a Google search on the differences.

I will share that Black sororities belong to an organization called The National Pan-Hellenic Council (NPHC), composed of nine historically Black sororities and fraternities and is often called the Divine 9. Many Divine 9 members were founded in the early 1900s and established mostly at HBCUs. You can also do further research on who belongs to the Divine 9. In addition to the Divine 9, there are several other councils as well. These councils govern other sororities, including Christian, professional, and music sororities. Look at the pros and cons below (these will vary based on your university) and answer the questions to help you think about whether joining is right for you.

JOINING SORORITIES

PROS
- Connecting with others and building community
- Creating lifelong friendships
- Community services and volunteer work
- Visibility
- Potential leadership opportunities
- Gaining skills
- Boosting confidence

JOINING SORORITIES

CONS
- The potential of being hazed, bullied, beaten, abused, and assaulted
- Possible peer pressure and influence to be promiscuous
- Expensive to join and costly to keep up
- Requires a LOT of your time and possibly conflicts with study schedules
- Potential sleep deprivation, poor nutrition, and physical health
- Destroying your reputation, losing identity, and becoming prideful
- Possible influence and peer pressure to partake in drugs/alcohol and other behaviors you normally wouldn't have

ASK YOURSELF THE FOLLOWING:
1. Does this organization's mission align with my values?

2. Will being a member of this organization give me something to be proud of?

3. Will I be able to prioritize my studies before the organization?

4. Can I handle the commitment, cost, and time that this organization will require of me?

5. Why do I want to join this organization?

6. Can I accomplish my (why) reason for pledging **outside of** this organization?

7. Do any symbols, practices, spiritual components, and gods associated with Divine 9 organizations contradict my faith, religion, and beliefs?

Joining clubs and organizations is a personal decision. I hope you make well-thought-through decisions that you can be proud of for years to come. Your choices should be for you and not anyone else. I say this personally: I've witnessed people only join organizations and clubs because their friends did. I knew people who were so committed to their organization or club that they prioritized the organization over their studies. Consequently, they had to stay in school for another year or two to graduate. This was because the club/organization required so much of their time, causing them to fail classes because they prioritized the club/organization over graduating.

Specifically, regarding Greek organizations, much of the community service is admirable and necessary. All the pros are obvious. However, it's the cons that I must warn you about. These apply to Greek and non-Greek organizations like band, SGA, and any clubs for that matter. I've known people to take out extra loans to cover costs; I've known people who experienced beatings, were humiliated, and became slaves to others in the organization. And lastly, I've heard stories and knew girls who compromised their values, doing things they didn't plan to do to be a part of an organization or to get the attention of guys in frat organizations. This happens all the time on many college campuses. The negative pressures associated with college overall can be hard but not impossible to overcome.

Just always remember that you are in school to graduate, gain skills, and land or create a life beyond college that you'll be proud to talk about and enjoy. So be careful not to devote more time to any organization or club that compromises your studies, identity, faith, or values. Lastly, if you do join clubs or organizations, do not allow them to define you. Keep balanced and focused.

VISITING HOME

I wanted to add this section because it's an important part of your transition into adulthood. Going home will never be the same as it was before you left. This is because as you begin to change, your parents and the home base you knew will also change.

Think about it like this. By the time you have your first visit back home (if you moved away), you will have gone from your family and old routines for close to four months. Most students usually return home by Thanksgiving after completing midterms and exams. Although you will still be a teenager, you will also be used to living independently.

This transition will still be similar if you're not living on campus. In your late teens, you're not quite a grown adult, and you're likely still depending on your parents' support in one way or another, which may continue even after turning 21. And listen, with that support will come some level of input in and about your life. Living on your own may make you feel like you're already grown, but in actuality, you're still growing.

I remember visiting home with my boyfriend during my junior year of college. On that visit, I felt like my mother was still treating me like a fifteen-year-old. It was weird and embarrassing to me for him to watch this. However, I wasn't grown grown, but at the same time, I was used to doing what I wanted without her input.

This transition can be tough because, for the most part, our parents will always see us (in some form) as their baby. This sometimes makes it hard for them to accept that we're growing up, have lived out in the world, and are making decisions for ourselves on our own.

As you start to gain more exposure, meet new people, and mentally develop, you'll start to remove the pedestals associated with your parents' titles. You will begin to see them as people, which can be either humorous, cool, or terrifying. For example, the moment you get to know and see Debra as Debra vs. your mother, it's a game changer.

When we see our parents as Momma or Daddy, this places an expectation and the idea that he or she should know certain things. For instance, looking at them through the parent lens, you'll more likely think they know what they're doing and have it all together. However, when you learn to see your parents as Debra and Mike, you'll see that Debra ain't so good with money and Mike has a short temper.

You'll also discover things about other trusted adults that you've put on a pedestal as a kid and that Auntie Tasha is really impulsive and insecure. But when you see your people under their titles, they can do no wrong and always know what's best.

I don't share this for you to go around looking upside your parents' head with judgmental eyes, but more so to anticipate that as you grow, you will see them differently. I hope that seeing them differently allows you to extend more grace to their humanity.

As humans, we all have shortcomings. Those are often revealed in hindsight as we grow while in relationships with others. You may also feel isolated and ostracized when you return home, especially if you are a first-generation student. I've seen this happen so many times. It happens because the more you grow and get exposed to new things, other cultures, and different experiences, this doesn't mean your family has or will. As a result, it can be challenging to connect with family and friends who aren't growing at a faster pace as you are, due to being in college.

Your intellect, vocabulary, communication, and social skills will increase, which is good! So please don't let anyone make you feel small for growing and changing. You should always be changing for the good. Good change denotes growth. I also want to touch on handling family adversities while in college. You may or may not be faced with these challenges, but in case you are, here's some food for thought.

ADVERSITIES AT HOME WHILE IN COLLEGE

My little sister got pregnant with her first child in my sophomore year. Meanwhile, my mother was battling an alcohol addiction, and my younger brother ran the streets.

Before leaving for college, my presence and role at home was the glue, logical thinker, and diplomat. I had always looked out for my siblings and helped my mother when I could. I was the first to graduate high school and go away to college as well. I was sad about leaving my family then because I wanted to ensure my siblings were straight. However, I saw college as an opportunity to better support my family, so I left.

While away in school for the first two years, it pained me to call home and learn what my siblings were going through. It hurt because I was only nineteen years old, far away, and couldn't help like I wanted. Adversities at home were challenging, but also what kept me motivated to grind hard.

At one point, I took out additional college loan money to send home while working to support my family as much as possible. I'm sharing this story with you because I wish I had known back then that it wasn't my responsibility to take care of my home. If I had known this then, I would have reduced anxiety and poor decisions.

Your sole job while in school (if you're not a mom) is to graduate, and you cannot do this effectively if you're taking on the weight of the world. You cannot pour from an empty cup if you have nothing to give. I do not say anything to discourage you from helping when you can and when there is an absolute emergency. I am, however, saying this to encourage you to prioritize first getting your footing and filling your cup. Then, you can give from the overflow of what you've filled yourself with.

Be wary of emotional manipulation from anyone that may make you feel like you have to save them. Pay attention to patterns of behaviors that get people in trouble in the first place. Someone else's irresponsibility does not have to be your crisis. Get into a habit of always empathizing with those you love who are going through it, and give it to God.

Sincerely pray for your loved ones, not as an option or a mention, but as a first resort. If prayer is all you have to give, trust that you've given them the absolute very best, and it's really up to God to change their circumstances and help them—not you. It is not your responsibility to save people. Help when you can and make peace to free up your emotional energy to finish your degree!

WAYS TO SET BOUNDARIES WITH YOUR LOVED ONES

Setting healthy boundaries with loved ones can be a big deal. Self-care is about setting boundaries. Setting boundaries with loved ones, especially parents can help reduce anger or resentment as we grow into adulthood. Our parents and loved ones should respect our decisions, voices, and perspectives, even if there is a difference of opinion or priorities.

Emotional manipulation, like pulling the "I brought you into this world" card when sharing your perspective, isn't cool at all. Your ideals are valid as long as you're utilizing healthy communication strategies and are respectful in your delivery.

As you grow into adulthood, you will need your own space to feel seen as an adult and capable of making decisions independently. Healthy boundaries include respecting each other's time, space, and perspective. However, this isn't always the case, hence a need for establishing boundaries, especially if you're having challenges with older loved ones respecting you. Here are a few tips to help set boundaries with parents and loved ones.

IDENTIFY WHAT HURTS
Identify your vulnerable areas, limits, and capacity with them. What makes you uncomfortable or irked?

PRAY
Pray for them and speak with trusted friends and others who can encourage you with wisdom.

SAY NO
Say no and give yourself space from them when you need it. If you stick around while irritated, you're likely to go off. So, cool off with some distance.

AVOID CONFLICT
Avoid conflict whenever you can if you feel it coming. Don't take the bait if they keep trying you or if the conversation isn't going anywhere.

BE DIRECT
Be direct yet mindful of tone when communicating your feelings. They may run over or manipulate you if you tiptoe or are too passive.

LET GO
Let go of any guilt associated with creating and enforcing boundaries with your loved ones and parents. As long as you remain respectful, you're good. You would be doing yourself a disservice and violating your own self-care by not upholding your boundaries.

ACCEPT
You may have to accept the fact that they will not change, and it's not your job to change them. You can only change you.

CHAPTER TWELVE
LIFE BEYOND COLLEGE
CAREER READINESS

Preparing for your senior year of college and transition beyond will be a bit similar but also different from your high school process. Only this time, the stakes and responsibility levels are higher, which is why taking those first few years in college seriously is important, especially if you want a comfortable life after graduation.

Much like the start of this book with that junior/senior year checklist, this chapter will also have checklists filled with resources, tips, and a few points to ponder as you prepare for adulting.

These four years in college will not only fly by but will also have a similar pattern. For example, in chapter 7, we broke down the components of college semesters and how the overall process is a rinse and repeat, consisting of class, classwork, reading, studying, and homework. Between these items will be events, parties, fun stuff, life, and holiday breaks, followed by spring and summer break and the following year. See the following.

Strategy, discipline, balance, and focus is the name of the game to do well and everything else previously discussed in this book. Seriously, if you utilize wisdom and apply what you've learned, you will come out on top! Wisdom is the application of knowledge. It's no use to learn something and not apply it. Make sense?

TIPS FOR MAKING THE MOST OF YOUR SENIOR YEAR

1. Revisit your grad plan, ensuring you're on track with the credits needed to graduate. Try to keep your load easy, if possible. Work closely with your advisors (academic and financial) to make sure you don't have any balances or holds on your account and are in good standing.

2. Are you considering, or does your field require grad school? If so, you'll need to look for grad schools and prepare for that application process.

3. No matter what, keep those grades up. Even if you have senioritis, you must push through because you are in the home stretch.

4. Intern, shadow professionals, and volunteer as much as possible to gain more professional experience.

5. Work closely with your campus career placement office and ask your professors and department chairs for opportunities they may know about.

6. Get letters of recommendation from professors, bosses, and faculty members.

7. Look for career and job fair opportunities.

8. Get a professional résumé and cover letter done. If your major or field permits your work to be displayed, put

together a portfolio of your work. For example, if you're into photography, a portfolio is an album of your images.

9. Create a list of companies you may be interested in and keep checking their website/LinkedIn pages for upcoming opportunities.

10. Clean up your social media/digital fingerprints and create or update your LinkedIn.

COLLEGE SENIOR YEAR CHECKLIST

- Be sure you get the approval from your advisor that you are cleared with credits to graduate that semester.

- Fill out the graduation application.

- Take graduation photos and send out save-the-dates to families.

- Order graduation announcements or design them yourself on Canva or other apps to save money. There are lots of templates out there.

- Keep your grades up and look for fellowship opportunities.

- Make sure you don't have outstanding fees with your apartment or financial aid.

- If you receive mail, go ahead and temporarily forward it to a relative or parents' home until you find a place.

- Make a list of all resources in the career center to help save money. See what they offer: jobs, databases, software, career fairs, networking events, etc.

- See if your alumni office offers short-term health insurance or car insurance as you prepare to exit school.

- Get all contact info for professors, friends, and references.

- Consider doing an online sale of things and books you don't want. Consider keeping books in your major if you're looking for work in your field.

NETWORKING/MENTORS/ADVOCATES

We talked about the power of networking in chapter 10 in the community building section. I can imagine that you've now grasped how important networking and relationships are. Remember, it's who you know that can get you in the door, and what you know that will keep you there. People are not created to live on islands; everyone got to where they are in their careers, work, and life with S-U-P-P-O-R-T! Don't let anyone tell you differently. We all need someone and are all connected to each other in one way or another.

We cross paths on a day-to-day basis with people who can add much value to our lives. We also can add value to the life of others as well. I believe the Lord orchestrates our paths, contacts, contracts, encounters, opportunities, and connections to cross. Whether you're a believer or not, you won't get to where you want to be alone.

Behind every successful Black woman is a story filled with a tribe of others supporting, rooting for, and cheering her on. Maybe these tribes were invisible and not in the forefront, but they were present at critical times and places on the journey.

Sometimes, it's the stranger who compliments you on a difficult day or that college counselor who helped you straighten out your financial aid situation. Perhaps it will be a professor who believes in you, or a Black woman sitting in on your panel job interview who will advocate for you behind closed doors and help you get the job.

Whoever these godsends will be, you will need them, and they are out there. So, let's cultivate our networking skills to find them. You'll need to network and build genuine mutual relationships for tremendous success.

WHAT NETWORKING IS AND WHAT IT AIN'T

Networking is not about what others can do for you. It is not a "what you can get and how you can benefit" mentality. Networking is offering service, mutually beneficial support, and cultivating genuine relationships. The more you give and serve, the more you will get back in return.

Serving others lays a strong foundation and provides a more natural way of connecting with individuals to build your community. It is also an opportunity to display your value. BTW, I am not suggesting that you be the only one doing the giving; instead, switch your mind to giving vs. receiving.

TIPS FOR NETWORKING AND IDENTIFYING MENTORS AND ADVISORS

1. Research and look for mentoring programs to apply to.

2. Take note and make a list of women you admire that you have access to. These can be women in the community, on campus, at your job, church, etc.

3. Be intentional with your positioning and efforts and organic in the approach. You'll know and feel if it's a vibe with someone who can mentor you. This is if you have access to her. If you don't know her personally, ask to meet for coffee and learn her story. Everyone loves to talk about themselves.

4. Be consistent and selective. I do not suggest stretching yourself thin or putting yourself in obligatory situations. Pick a few women to connect with and be intentional about those. This means don't try to build new relationships with twenty women simultaneously. If you're in a nursing program and you spot a woman who is already working in her career, get to know her and be consistent in developing a relationship. Building relationships takes time and intentionality.

5. Join groups and clubs to meet others. Find out who the people you are connected to know. Don't be afraid to network with your peers as you're both climbing to the top so you can support and help each other along the journey. I got my first job at a news station because a producer who came across my résumé was friends with someone I interned with, and she hired me on the spot without interviewing. You never know who knows whom, which is also why keeping a great reputation is important.

6. Speak, smile, and be friendly and inviting. You never know who's watching you. Your demeanor and energy will tell it all. Be what you would want to attract.

7. Engage on social media/LinkedIn with other professionals in your industry.

8. Volunteer and get to know people through your service. Remember, it's who you know that can get you in.

9. Flat out ask if someone is willing to be a mentor to you.

CAREER READINESS

At the college level, career readiness consists of thinking through your plan of action for life after graduation. If you're aiming to be a doctor or in the medical profession, you will need to continue school. You will also need to continue school if you plan on getting a master's degree as well. The timing it takes to reach your long-term goals is totally up to you. However, if you decide to continue pursuing school, I recommend keeping going, especially if you have loans. Since you are already in college mode, you may find this to be easier

RÉSUMÉ AND INTERVIEWING TIPS

RÉSUMÉS
- Have this professionally reviewed, and be sure to use action verbs and language that highlight your successes.
- Create different résumés for different jobs. Make sure your résumé makes sense for what you are applying for, and make sure the résumé highlights your transferable skills.
- Apply with a résumé that reflects language that is directly from the job posting.
- Keep your LinkedIn and portfolio that reflects your résumé skills updated.

JOB APPLYING
- Be honest and do not lie on your applications. This will come back and bite you.
- Leverage your communities and networks and ask them

about opportunities.
- Create a cover letter or personal statement about who you are and what value you can add to better sell yourself.
- Keep all your professional profiles updated.
- Ask trusted people for recommendations and references.

WHEN INTERVIEWING & AFTER
- Research people you'll interview with. See what you can find about them. Look to see if you have anything in common to build a connection with them.
- Sell yourself, speaking confidently about your skills, and don't hold back.
- Be yourself and be honest about what you have to offer.
- Remember, you are the prize, too, so it's a privilege for them to have you.
- Be prepared to respond to questions using the S.T.A.R method (see S.T.A.R. example below).
- Ask questions about the position to show that you care and are interested.
- Send a follow-up thank-you email or handwritten card one to two days after interviewing. You can reiterate skills or share anything you forgot to mention in your follow-up.

USE THE STAR METHOD
- Have a previous job **Situation** example prepared. This situation can be from class, in school, life, or another job. Make sure it's relevant to what you're asked.
- Share the **Tasks** you were given in previous roles or the situations that you're using.
- Share what **Actions** you took regarding the tasks.
- Be able to share the **Result** of what happened (good or bad). If you share a bad result, be sure to talk about what you learned and walked away with.

ACCEPTING OR DECLINING OFFERS

- Research similar titles/positions in the city to see what the pay is to ensure the compensation is fair.
- Remember, statistically, Black women are underpaid, so be sure to always request your worth after you've done proper research!
- If they offer you the job under the amount you hoped for, you can always counteroffer, asking for more. There is never a penalty for this.
- Consider the full-package benefits (EAP, 401k matching, etc.). These may actually add up to the amount you requested, even if the base salary is a bit lower.
- Get everything in writing and your money upfront. Don't allow them to say something like after a year, we will pay you ____ amount. Get everything in writing for proof.
- If you're asking for more money, be able to substantiate your ask. This means you're able to demonstrate your worth and why you deserve to be paid. Show them vs. telling them. You can show them with your GPA, projects you lead, recommendation letters, and portfolios.
- Keep positive relationships with all recruiters and people you interviewed with, even if you don't get the job. I've had people interview me for one thing but recommend me for something different.

TRANSFERABLE SKILLS

These are skills you can easily transfer from one job to another. You may need to lean on these as you exit college unless you've had a few jobs while in school. Transferable skills may be soft skills like collaboration and problem-solving or hard skills like data analytics or coding. See examples.

TRANSFERABLE SKILLS/VOCABULARY

GENERAL
Organized
Team oriented
Self-motivated
Creative
Adaptive
Flexible

IT/ TECH
Coding and programming
Social media management
Video editing
Web design
AI creations

MANAGEMENT/LEADERSHIP
Networking
Leading others
Decision-making
Planning/organized
Project management
Dependable

ADMINISTRATIVE
Data entry
Computer skills/typing
Microsoft Office
Critical thinking
Planning/filing
Organizing
Attention to detail

LIFE BEYOND COLLEGE
CAREER READINESS

TRANSFERABLE SKILLS/VOCABULARY

COMMUNICATION SKILLS
Content creation
Writing and storytelling
Active listening and social media management
Being on camera
Public speaking and presenting

INTERPERSONAL SKILLS
Conflict resolution
Client and customer service
Motivating and encouraging others
Empathic and kind
Good with people and coaching

COUNTEROFFER
A counteroffer is a response to an offer from a potential new employer. This is when you respond to the job's offer with a different request, usually higher than originally offered. For example, Delta Airlines offers you a full-time job starting at $40k for base salary plus bonus, but you counter and say you are willing to accept the offer if they can bump that base salary up to $50k. Please remember that this isn't bad, and most hiring managers are willing to negotiate anyway. Always check the average salary for the position and know what your ask is. Also, consider the wage gaps and statistics around Black women being underpaid. Therefore, I recommend your counter to go up $10k-$20k if you decide to counter. Being fresh out of college and lacking experience may come with a lower salary, but knowing the average amount for college grads and selling your value may warrant asking for more. You should always request a bit more and let them talk you down to a number

you're actually comfortable with.

BASE SALARY VS. SALARY

Your salary is your paycheck and compensation for working. The base is usually the flat amount that excludes additional pay like bonuses, overtime, benefits, and awards. Those extra things will reflect your salary as a whole. This is why knowing the difference is important. Think about my previous example: Delta Airlines offers a base salary of $40k, but because of all the bonuses, benefits, awards, and possible overtime, that salary jumps to $60k. Do you see why knowing the difference can help you decide whether to counter the offer?

BENEFITS

These are nonmonetary compensations that you will receive in addition to your salary. Some jobs may pay low but have great benefits that may mean more to you than the additional money. For example, the Delta Airlines offer. Perhaps you're not too thrilled about it, but one of the benefits of working for that company may be free flights. This may be something that keeps your attention.

INTERVIEW TIPS

- List out and know your top qualities and skills and how they can transfer into whatever role you are applying for.

- Be able to sell yourself to the employer. Why should they hire you?

- Be able to communicate why you applied and what was appealing about this job to you.

- Practice your responses with a friend or with yourself on Zoom.

- Be on time if the interview is in person (15 minutes early).

- Bring your updated résumé and portfolio with you.

- Put your phone on silent.

- Dress appropriately and be very professional, even if the interview is on Zoom.

- If on Zoom, please check your equipment, microphone, and lighting, and make sure your background is appropriate.

- Prepare questions for them as well. This is a two-way street; as bad as you want the job, it also needs to make sense for your life.

SAMPLE INTERVIEW QUESTIONS TO ASK FUTURE EMPLOYERS

- What are the day-to-day responsibilities for this role?

- Who is your ideal candidate, and what characteristics does she have?

- Who does this role report to, and what is that person's leadership style like?

- How does your company help to ensure diverse, inclusive, and equitable hires and employee culture?

- If I got this role, how would performance be measured?

- What do you like best and least about working here?

- How will the person in this role be set up for success?

- What is your hiring timeline?

- Have I said anything so far that gives you pause or that I can elaborate on further?

ADULTING AND PLANNING THE NEXT

By the end of your four years in college, you will have grown tremendously! I guarantee you'll look nothing like that nervous high school student at the start of this book, and if you did what you were supposed to do, you will be more than prepared for your next. As you face the prospect of leaving school, you'll automatically enter into a new set of adulting tasks that can feel like a lot. While it may feel like a lot, you'll need to remember that you are prepared and divinely guided. God is with you and has already ordered your steps, little sister.

That transition after college requires coming to grips with the difference between obtaining instant results vs. the wait of the real world. Yep, you read that right. In the real world, you will have to wait and wait frequently.

For example, you can do everything right, study hard, and receive an A in school. Receiving an A is an instant result of the work you put in. On the other hand, in the real world, you can do everything right, work really hard, and still not see results, at least not right away.

In life after school, things are a process, and there is so much more to juggle and be responsible for. You may begin a life of nine-to-five work, fifty weeks a year, without the open schedule and flexibility you had in college. You'll need to pay rent, bills and be solely responsible for everything.

Success in the real world may also feel a bit harder to obtain, and the competition is steeper. This is why resilience is important. We talked about resilience in chapter 9. Remember, resilience is the ability to endure or recover quickly from challenges, difficulties, and hard times. You will need the skill of being resilient in the real world, and I would be setting you up for failure if I did not tell you this truth. Below are a few things to consider postgraduation.

- Where will you live? Is there an option to go back home? If so, can you tolerate being back as an adult, and how long will you stay?

- How will you find a place to live? Can you afford to live solo, or will you get a roommate? If you decide on a roomie, how will you find them?

- Can you afford to hold out for a job you want in your field, or should you take something to pay the rent?

- What will be your living expenses? How will you be able to afford them?

- Do you need to get a car, or can you use public transit?

- Have you thought about some of the financial risks associated with college loan debt or started thinking through your plan?

- How will you repay student loans after your six-month grace period ends?

- Are you planning to enroll in grad school? If so, have you identified where, and if in another state, are you prepared to move?

- Do you understand that having an education doesn't protect you from inequalities? Are you aware that you may face intersectionality (racism, sexism, microaggressions, and discrimination) as a Black woman when starting your career?

- Are you comfortable counteroffering if need be and confident negotiating job benefits? Retirement? Healthcare? Insurance?

- Will you be okay if things don't go as you planned right away? Will you keep showing up and giving yourself grace?

STUDENT LOANS

Chapter 5 covered loan types, budget samples, and ways to financially prepare for life after college. We talked about different loan types, including:

- **Direct Subsidized Loans** are for eligible undergraduate students to help cover college or career school. The Department of Education pays the interest on these loans while you are in school.

- **Direct Unsubsidized Loans** are for eligible undergraduate, graduate, and professional students. Eligibility is not based on financial need. You are responsible for paying the interest on these loans while in school.

The subsidized loan allows for a six-month grace period before you have to actually start making payments. This is why scholarships are invaluable. Those six months will fly by, and it's not guaranteed you will land a job right away. As best as we can, we want to eliminate the threat of potential unnecessary stress associated with loan companies harassing you for their money. And yes! They will hound you.

My goal in this section is to encourage you to minimally have a plan, keep any accrued debt under control, and preserve your credit score while not allowing money owed to stress you out too badly.

Remember that statistically, Black women graduate with more debt. Black students take out the most student loans to pay for college, holding almost twice as much debt as white peers. Out of women undergraduate borrowers, the average Black woman has the most student debt, averaging under $42,000 one year after graduation. This information can help families think through and plan to pay for college.

Below are a few things to consider regarding your loans after college.

1. Do not ignore loans, loan companies, or payments. Ignoring problems will NEVER make them go away. Avoidance only worsens matters and can impact your taxes and everything else.

2. Know exactly how much you borrowed and who has your loan, and keep track of all your details for each loan.

3. You may qualify for help with payments, including zero or low payments, based on how much money you make or don't make. Call your loan lenders and find out what repayment options you are eligible for. Pick the right payment options. You can log on to studentaid.gov for more detailed info regarding options.

4. Know the dates of your grace periods if you have other loans outside the subsidized loan.

5. Repay the loan if you can and start with the larger loan first, creating a system to get it off your back.

6. You can also consider merging multiple loans together to make one payment. This is called consolidating loans. First, consider the pros and cons before deciding which way to go. Please look this up!

7. Consider working in fields that support loan forgiveness. Most public servant fields offer this, such as government jobs, nonprofit, and public service jobs.

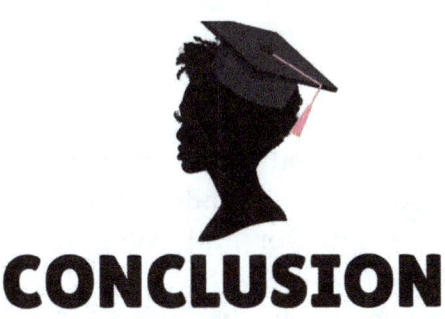

CONCLUSION

The college process, from start to finish, can be an incredible experience and time in your life. It's full of possibilities, excitement, learning opportunities, and character-building, ultimately defining and shaping the type of woman you'll be in life.

College Bound: A Black Girl's Guide is important because most mainstream college prep materials aren't explicitly speaking to you or addressing your unique challenges and issues. When these issues are not mentioned or considered, it sends messages of invisibility and invalidation, further exacerbating the problem and leaving you, as a Black girl, underprepared for your professional journeys.

It is my prayer that this book and every lesson in it will help to serve as a guide for a successful and balanced future.

Dear Black girl, your voice, perspective, and contributions to this planet are so valuable. God created you for things far greater than you can ever imagine. You have everything you need (on the inside of you) to be successful and everything you were created for. But you'll have to feed, nurture, and use it. What's inside of you is no good if it isn't growing, being stimulated, stretched, or let out.

Let your light shine BRIGHT, feed what's on the inside of you by looking for learning opportunities, reading, intimacy with your Creator, and staying committed to growing. The world and other young Black girls need what you have to offer. They'll need you in a position to mentor, support, and be a shining example of Black excellence that gives them hope and something to aspire to.

It's been said and proven that complacency among Blacks is the key to white supremacy. White supremacy is a belief that white people are a superior and better race and, therefore, should dominate society.

We know this isn't true because God created everyone equal, with no race being superior to another. However, there are systems, laws, behaviors, and beliefs in our country that say otherwise. This is why educating yourself is so important. I don't want you to be naïve or caught off guard by adversities you may face in life.

Because representation matters, you must know that Black women are highly educated. According to the American Association of University Women, among Black students attending college and universities, Black women earn over 64% of bachelor's degrees, about 72% of master's degrees, and almost 66% of doctoral, medical, and dental degrees.[15]

These statistics are important, so you'll know how educated women in the culture are. Your graduation and success increase these stats, and it helps to dispel inaccurate misconceptions and negative portrayals of us in mainstream culture. What's cool is that it gives younger girls looking up to you something to aspire to. So, by all means, avoid complacency and learn as much as possible for yourself, your community, and your future.

Remember that just because you'll be educated doesn't mean you won't face inequities. You'll have to be fully aware of the risks of racial workplace bullying, sexism, tone policing, labels of being angry, aggressive, or experiencing

---

[15] "Fast Facts: Women of Color in Higher Ed," AAU, https://www.aauw.org/resources/article/fast-facts-woc-higher-ed/.

microaggressive behaviors toward you. Your education won't shield you from any of this. You may enter spaces where you are the most educated, talented, and qualified but also the most overlooked. Consider how you will handle this.

Also, consider the entrepreneurial opportunities you will imagine and create to build wealth and gain financial freedom. There is lots to think about, and because you're privy, you will be far ahead.

I'll close with this. There's an old quote rumored to have come from The Willie Lynch speech on the making of a slave that says, "If you want to hide something from a Black person, put it in a book." The quote is insinuating that Black people won't or don't read.

I do believe that reading not only funds your mental but it's power. A lack of access to knowledge, money, wisdom, and strategy is one of the biggest downfalls in our communities. This is why I wrote this book, and I'm thrilled that you've picked it up and are also almost finished reading it. I'm confident that because you're educating yourself, you will help break barriers and bridge gaps in racial disparities in our country.

You are the future, Black girl. Never let anyone take your power or make you feel inferior because of your style, voice, hair texture, pizazz, or skin tone. The world needs you, all of you, and the **educated** and prepared version of you.

College is only a fraction of your life and a moment in time. Your college experience and how you handle it helps to set the tone for your future. As you master the skills of making healthy choices, setting boundaries, being responsible, time management, conflict resolution, communication, advocating for yourself, and implementing self-care, you will be the woman you set out to be, making a major difference in college, your community, and the culture, becoming a leading authority for life after high school and college.

PS. I believe in you; you've got this!

with love,
Coach Rahki Roberson

ABOUT THE AUTHOR

Rahkal Shelton Roberson is a proud HBCU alum, certified professional coach, career strategist, mentor, and college prep champion. She is the CEO of **Black Girl College Prep**, a college, life, and career-readiness service dedicated to equipping and building legacy-minded leaders. Rahkal is the author of Woosah: A Survival Guide for Women of Color Working in Corporate, Woosah Workplace Peace: 7 Keys to Obtaining a More Fulfilling Work Experience, and Dreams Bigger Than Texas: A Story of Faith, Perseverance, and Growth Into Womanhood. She is passionate about empowering millennial, first-gen, and Gen Z women, helping them make smart and strategic career-planning moves! Her leading approach is servant and transformational. She reaches clients on a heartfelt and personal level. Rahkal holds a bachelor's in radio, television, and film from Texas Southern University and a master's in media communications and training from Governors State University. Her uncanny ability to connect and educate is the foundation of her personal mission: serving, inspiring, and helping individuals confidently identify, own, and live out their God-given purpose. Her expertise has been highlighted in Forbes, HuffPost, WGN, VoyageATL, The Talk of Chicago, and Radio One. She and her husband, Dr. Joe L. Roberson, Jr., live in Atlanta, Georgia. Stay connected and learn more at www.rahkalshelton.com and www.blackgirlcollegeprep.com

www.ingramcontent.com/pod-product-compliance
Lightning Source LLC
Chambersburg PA
CBHW071223080526
44587CB00013BA/1480